Blazing *the* Freelance Trail

PROFESSIONAL PRACTICES FOR CREATIVE ENTREPRENEURS

Eric Holter

ILLUSTRATIONS BY BRIAN MILLER

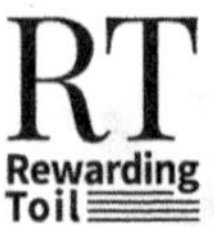

Rewarding Toil Publishing
Durham, NC, USA

Blazing the Freelance Trail

Copyright © 2019 by Eric Holter.
All Rights Reserved.

No part of this publication may be reproduced, stored in a retrieval system or transmitted, in any form or by any means—electronic, mechanical, photocopying, recording or otherwise—without prior written permission from the publisher, except for the inclusion of brief quotations in a review.

For information about this title or to order other books and/or electronic media, contact the publisher:
Rewarding Toil
www.rewardingtoil.com
sales@rewardingtoil.com

Library of Congress Control Number: In Process

ISBN: 978-1-7333139-0-2 (softcover)
        978-1-7333139-1-9 (eBook)
        978-1-7333139-2-6 (audio book)

Printed in the United States of America

Cover and Interior Design: 1106 Design
Cover and Interior Illustration: Brian Miller

Table of Contents

Acknowledgments ix

Preface xiii

Introduction 1
  A Word of Caution 1
  An Overview of the Path Ahead 2

Chapter 1: MONEY 9
  Dealing with Financial Realities is Required 10
    A Disdain of "Commercial" Art? 11
    Is Money Tainted? 12
    Is Profit Tainted? 13
    Profits Are Crucial for Freelancers 14
    The Beauty of Economic Benefits 15
    How Much Benefit? How Much Value? 17
  Establishing A Freelance Rate: A Harbinger of Things to Come 18
    Billing by the Hour Is a Losing Proposition 18
    A Rate That Serves Your Future 20

Chapter 2: MINUTES 21
  Managing a Business Means Making Decisions 22
    Measuring Every Minute 23
  Common Objections to Keeping Timesheets 23
    "Deadlines Kill Creativity" 23
    Be More Like Leonardo 24
    Overcoming Resistance to Time Tracking:
      Have a Long-Term Outlook 25

Measuring Time's Benefit to the Creative Process — 27
Making Use of Your Time Data — 28
Producing Quotes and Schedules — 28
Being Your Own Project Manager — 29
What Your Time Will Tell You — 30

Chapter 3: MARKETING — **33**
Marketing Out of the Ashes of Failure — 34
What is "Sales" and What is "Marketing" — 34
The Key to Marketing: Narrow Positioning — 35
The Bitter Pill of Narrow Positioning — 36
Positioning and the Artist's Dilemma — 37
Practical Benefits of Narrow Positioning — 37
What Narrow Positioning Does Not Mean — 39
Creative Advantages to Narrow Positioning — 40
A Sales Illustration of Marketing with a Narrow Positioning — 42
The Sales Experience of the Passive Generalist Position — 43
Contrast: The Sales Experience of the Narrowly
Positioned Expert — 44
Are There Any Alternatives? — 47
Limitations of Generalist Positioning — 48
Who Can Thrive Under Generalist Conditions? — 49
Trade-offs for the Generalist Practice — 50
Can You Endure Narrow Positioning? — 51

Chapter 4: MANAGEMENT — **53**
Two Common Mistakes When Heading Down the Hiring Path — 54
Hiring to Avoid Burnout — 55
Mistakes from Hiring from Success — 57
The Big "Step" of Hiring Your First Employee — 59
A Final Test Before Hiring — 60
No 50/50 Partnerships! — 60
Staying Small and Profitable by Learning to Say "No" — 61
Wearing All the Hats — 63

Table of Contents

A Lot to Take In   65

Chapter 5: MOTIVATION   **67**

Rewarding Toil   68
    A Higher Goal to Aim For   68
Deconstructing Artistic Motivation   69
    The Complicated Connection Between Work and Meaning   69
The Artist's Unique Relationship to Work   70
    The Connection Between Meaning and Work   71
    How Seeking Meaningful Work Can Collide with
      Our Pursuit of Happiness   72
Human Angst Revealed in Art History   75
    An Example from *The Cardboard Bernini*   75
You're Bringing Me Down, Man!   76
    Meaning Modified by the Span of Our Lives   76
    Meaning Modified by the Extent of Our Impact   77
Where Motivation Can Be Found   78
    Is Artistic Angst a Blessing or a Curse?   78
    Replacing the Pursuit of Meaning with the
      Pursuit of Goodness   80
    The Joys of Attaining Redirected Ends   81
Diagnosing Angst in Your Practice   82
    Added Benefits of an Adjusted Motivation   82

Gearing Up for the Path Ahead   **85**

Chapter 6: MANAGEMENT in Practice   **87**

How to Wear All the Hats Without Hiring   88
    The Production Role   89
    Administrative Roles   91
    Client Service Roles   95
    Marketing and New Business Roles   97
Tips for Disciplined Hat Swapping   99
Chapter 6: MANAGEMENT—Summary and Assignments   103

Chapter 7: MARKETING in Practice   **105**

A Sharper, More Effective Content Strategy   106

    The Wrong Kind of Content   106

    The Right Kind of Blog Content   107

    Benefits of a Focused Blog Strategy   107

Narrow Positioning Exercise   108

How Narrow Positioning Facilitates Prospecting   110

    Finding Prospects with LinkedIn   111

    An Additional Benefit to Prospecting with LinkedIn   111

Tools of the Marketing Trade   112

    Choosing a Customer Relationship Management system (CRM)   112

    Choosing an Email Marketing Platform   113

    Designing Your Marketing Workflow   114

On Networking   115

    Generalist Networking: Proceed with Caution   116

    Networking vs. Industry Conferences and Speaking Engagements   116

Chapter 7: MARKETING—Summary and Assignments   119

Chapter 8: MINUTES in Practice   **121**

How Much Time Do You Really Have?   122

    Billable Project Time (60%)   123

    Overhead Time (40%)   123

How to Plan Your Week   125

Tracking Every Minute   126

    Completeness and Accuracy   127

Logical Timesheet Categories   128

    The Importance of Project Phases   129

    Nonproject Phases   131

Project Coordination   133

Project Status and Completion Evaluations   134

    Which Budget to Measure Against?   135

Table of Contents

Choosing a Timekeeping System ... 136
Chapter 8: MINUTES—Summary and Assignments ... 137

Chapter 9: MONEY in Practice ... 139
What is Your Money Saying Right Now? ... 140
What Should Your Financial Targets Be? ... 140
   Profitability Calculator ... 142
What Should Your Target Rate Be? ... 146
Getting to Know Your Financial Instruments ... 148
Managing Your Cash Flow ... 152
   What Are Cash Flow Problems, Really? ... 153
The Cash Flow Spreadsheet ... 154
   Modeling Receivables in the Cash Flow Spreadsheet ... 155
   Planning Receipt of Milestone Invoices ... 156
   Earned vs. Unearned Revenue ... 157
   Modeling Expenses in the Cash Flow Spreadsheet ... 158
   Keeping the Cash Flow Spreadsheet Up-To-Date ... 160
Weekly Updating ... 162
   Maintaining the Cash Flow Spreadsheet Year over Year ... 162
Should You Just Hire a Bookkeeper? ... 163
Invoicing: Putting Weight on the Trust Bridge ... 164
Increasing Your Rates ... 165
   The Paralyzing Fear of Disappointing Clients ... 166
   Timing is Everything ... 167
   How to Bring Your Clients Along ... 168
Messages from Your Money ... 171
Chapter 9: MONEY—Summary and Assignments ... 173

Conclusion ... 175

Afterword ... 177

About the Author ... 179

Acknowledgments

This book is a synthesis of my experiences as a creative entrepreneur. Even as a high school student, my artistic endeavors were matched by my entrepreneurial bent. In my senior year, I quit my grocery store job and hung out a shingle as an artist available for commissions. And while that success was meager, it certainly outperformed my minimum-wage cashier job. Now, as I finish this manuscript, I'm just weeks from my fiftieth birthday. I've been engaged in one form or another in creative entrepreneurship going on four decades.

But while that time frame has offered me sufficient experiences to write a book like this, to think that the insights I offer in these pages are all from my individual experiences and personal reflections would be the height of arrogance. Bernard of Chartres wrote,

> *"We are like dwarfs on the shoulders of giants. We see more things than the ancients and things more distant, but it is due neither to the sharpness of our sight nor the greatness of our stature. It is simply because they have lent us their own."*

And so I offer these insights from my perch on the shoulders of others, acknowledging my debt. Bernard acknowledges our debt to "the ancients," rightly so, since we are all indebted to a long stream of cultural foundations, traditions, and profound opportunities that we did not create for ourselves. But it is also fitting to examine the personal giants, the people in our individual lives, who have contributed to the opportunities we've had to stand, and glimpse an insight or two.

I want to begin with the debt I owe to my Uncle Benny and Aunt Evie. They passed on decades ago, while I was just beginning to explore the freelance trail for the first time. But it was their estate that paid for my art education. Rhode Island School of Design is not cheap, and it was not cheap in the late eighties. Without that inheritance, I could never have even begun my journey. And while their estate paid my tuition, that only happened because of my parents. Why they thought their wacko, artsy teenage son should use this inheritance—*for an art education*—I can't fathom. But I hope that my successes over the years have honored that profound gift. And as I am now paying for my own children's college tuition, that gift is being paid forward to the next generation.

The path of the entrepreneur is winding, steep, hazardous, and stressful. And I would never have made it this far without the unmerited support and love of my wife Becca. She has continually surprised me with her trust as I've taken risks with multiple creative startups over the years. I am blessed with a wife who has faith, not in me, but in God, and then, on that basis, she trusts me enough to take this ride. She has endured my stresses, sleepless nights, financial pressures, uncertainties, and all the struggles of a creative startup.

When it comes to my business insights, I owe a huge debt to David C. Baker. I engaged him for business consulting in 2000. His advice transformed me from a completely lucky and clueless creative startup founder into a more deliberate and controlled business owner. It was a hard transition for a creative, but it was critical to the success of that company. Many of the core principles about positioning and financial benchmarks included in this book come from him.

I also want to thank many of the employees I've hired over the years who had a seat on the roller coaster along with me. This book is a synthesis of many experiences, and as is usually the case, we synthesize best from our failures than from our successes. And so those riding with me had to endure all the sharp turns, steep drops, and shaky tracks. They thought I was steering. Ha! In particular, I want to thank Mark O'Brien, to whom I sold Newfangled, who is still leading that firm.

Acknowledgments

He experienced the ride almost from the start, through the dot com bubble burst, and the catastrophic effects of 9/11 on the business world, and many other calamities. Chris Butler and Dave Mello are two other Newfangled veterans who stayed on the ride. I also want to thank my current business partner at Cuberis, Ray Parrish, who has entrusted me with running his firm, and rides along with me today.

Finally, I want to thank Nick Faber, a brilliant content strategist, writer, and producer, who helped shape this book from its stale original manuscript into a more engaging journey. His strategic editorial help, and content editing significantly improved the final result.

Preface

The creative profession is driven by artistic passion. Artists transform the ordinary into the extraordinary. This drive, combined with talent and skill, produces awe-inspiring works of creative genius. Can you imagine how bland and boring life would be without the beauty and pleasure creativity brings to our world? Creative contributions are not just found in museums and art galleries. All manner of products, tools, and entertainment are shaped and formed through the creative profession. Take, for example, the letters you're reading right now. These shapes are part of a typeface called *Alegreya* designed by Juan Pablo del Peral at the Huerta Tipográfica, an Argentinian type foundry. We often take beautiful things like typefaces for granted. But Juan labored over the shapes, counter spaces, balance, and form of each letter you're reading. He had to spend time crafting every character: upper case, lower case, normal, italic, and bold. He drew every numeral, every punctuation character, even the ones we hardly ever use like "§" and "ʃ." Thanks, Juan.

When we walk down the grocery store aisles or peruse bookstore shelves, we don't think about the hours of toil that went into each product's packaging, or every book cover's design. But each one is the result of someone's talent, time, and labor. Designers know that behind every one of those products was a lengthy and thoughtful design process. One of the proper effects of good design is to glorify the virtues of a product in such a way that the design itself recedes, not calling too much attention to itself, allowing the product's benefits to emerge. There is an elegance to good design that does not need to shout. But getting to that effective and elegant solution takes a lot of work and skill. Every design process is a labor of love. If you want to get a behind-the-scenes peek at the kind of artistic labor that goes into something as common as the movies we enjoy, check out a few samples from *Every Frame a Painting* on YouTube.

The design process itself is a laborious effort. But when you consider the business side to creativity, you introduce additional challenges—challenges that the typical creative mind or creative spirit find even more daunting. The professional creative process often includes frustrations, failures, setbacks, and client conflicts along the way. Behind every expression of design that we encounter every day are countless hours of craftsmanship, labor, and managerial frustration.

Every product, or clothing item, or album cover, or book, or magazine, or website we visit was created by someone. What's more, most of the time, these objects integrate the work of multiple artists. Consider a simple cookbook. It was designed by a book designer but uses typefaces, photographs, and illustrations provided by several different artists and designers. What a wonderful service artists do for each of us—how greatly they augment and improve our everyday lives.

Unfortunately, artists rarely receive a proper reward for bringing such beauty into the world. Their compensation falls woefully short of the time it took to produce their work. They give more than they receive. Not that anyone is defrauding them. In their passion to create, they can't help but to pursue the most aesthetically pleasing product they can. This passion overrides their profit motive. They enjoy staying fixed in the creative zone. They love to craft, experiment, and explore as they perfect their work. They do this to the exclusion of more fundamental business necessities, like working within a budget and schedule, or managing their books regularly, or marketing their practice. Their clients, and we the consumers, benefit from this imbalance. But are we taking advantage of the creative drive to the detriment of the artists themselves?

This imbalance is not fair, but it is not unjust. Artists willingly (though perhaps unwisely) enter into agreements to produce work for fees agreeable to both parties. It's not until much later that an artist realizes that they were underpaid, sometimes so much later that they cannot even pin down which projects got them into financial trouble in the first place. Disinterest (or creative distraction) keeps them from the technical business processes that might have revealed the causes of their eventual financial stress and lack of profitability. And so this cycle continues. And since almost all artists fall into this trap, the entire creative services market has been distorted by clients trained to expect unrealistic pricing levels. When unwitting or creatively-distracted artists and designers flood the market with underpriced services, price expectations end up conforming to the rates creatives willingly accept—prices subsidized by their artistic passions.

If this imbalance is ever to be rectified, it's going to have to start with changes in the creative profession first. Creative entrepreneurs need to treat their talent as the valuable commodity that it is. No client is going to voluntarily pay more than they have to. Unless you, as the artist, demand the higher fee, and demonstrate why you're worth it, the market will not change. So creative services professionals have to change the market. It starts with you. You have to stop selling yourself short.

This book exists to help creative professionals gain new business management habits for their creative service businesses so that they receive the rewards they are due for all their artistic efforts. Fixing things that are broken is never easy. If you let yourself get out of physical shape, the path back to fitness will require hunger and strenuous exercise. If you let your business get out of fiscal shape, the path to health will require an investment of time, effort, and yes, some pain.

Creating beautiful things can, indeed, be its own reward. It is the core reward most artists desire. But unless your creative practice is also sustainable (profitable), even the reward of creative satisfaction will likely get tarnished and spoiled under the stresses that come from mounting financial failure. It's not impossible to fix this. It can be done. It will take some work, some toil, some good old fashioned perseverance. But you can do it.

Introduction

A Word of Caution

This book is a guide to professional creative entrepreneurship.

By professional, I mean that you've decided to pursue creativity as a career, not a hobby or temporary experiment.

By creative, I include all manner of disciplines in the creative arts: graphic designers, illustrators, photographers and videographers, copywriters, and creative strategists and consultants. Even fine artists can benefit from this book, though the majority of the principles are geared toward contract-based commercial art.

And by entrepreneurship, I mean creative individuals who are still in the process of establishing their practice. That might be day one following a decision to launch off on a freelance career. It might be a freelance content strategist who's busier than ever, but can't figure out why they keep having cash flow problems. It might be the freelancer who's so busy that they're considering bringing on an employee or two. Or it could be a small design firm with several employees that continues to have business development or profitability problems.

In all these cases, the effort to establish a new practice, or transition from freelance into a profitable firm, carries with it all the entrepreneurial challenges of starting any business. Unfortunately, unlike investor-funded startups, creative professionals rarely take on business partners, who, along with their money, bring business expertise, insight, and managerial resources to give startups their best chance for success.

Not only do creative entrepreneurs lack resources for professional advice, there's also something baked into the creative mind-set that revolts from basic business fundamentals such as reviewing financials, tracking cash flow, measuring and managing time, and engaging in effective marketing. This double whammy of lack of experienced advice and the disinclination toward business matters cripples the creative enterprise and leads to the demise of many creative businesses. This book will address both dynamics, and try to make up for the lack of real world entrepreneurial advice for creative startups.

Before we get into the business particulars for whatever sort of freelance practice you are planning, or where you are in your journey, you need to understand that this is going to be difficult. This is not your typical lightweight "how to get started" guide. You're going to need to get ready for an entirely new perspective.

If you've ever watched the popular show *Shark Tank*, you know that the investors ask tough questions. When founders don't know their numbers, or when their numbers reveal serious weakness, they're going to get called on it. Likewise, some of the principles and practices described in this book are going to reveal all the weak spots in your business plan, starting with the reality that you probably don't even have a plan.

But I am assuming that you are serious about starting a long-term, professional, creative career—either as a successful solo practitioner, or eventually as a profitable firm.

Either way, if you want to gain success, stability, profitability, and control over your work, and if you're ready to boldly declare that you're starting a creative *business*, then read on.

An Overview of the Path Ahead

This book is organized around five subject areas: Money, Minutes, Marketing, Management, and Motivation. In the first half of the book,

I will introduce you to each of these facets on a conceptual level. This will allow you to reflect on your own challenges and goals as you prepare to build your business. In the second half, you will learn the practical applications of each topic.

The crucial first leg of the journey will be an uphill climb, but no matter how difficult it might feel, you need to make a commitment to reaching the peak—the chapter on "Motivation." Think of this chapter as the summit of the mountain, offering you a chance to rest and take in the vistas ahead of you. From this vantage point, you will be able to see the landscape of your business with new breadth and clarity.

You may need a breather after that, because you won't be heading back down the mountain on the same path that brought you up. You're going to need to blaze a new trail down the other side of the mountain. And so we'll revisit each subject in reverse order, applying everything we learned on the ascent to your business with practical tools and instruments.

There is a logical progression for why these subject areas follow one another the way that they do. However, that order does not necessarily reflect *the priority* of each of these topics. They all interrelate and build on each other, but depending on your situation, one aspect may have a higher implementation priority for you than the others. So after you read through the first five chapters, gaining an overview of the issues and how they interrelate, you might choose to focus your time asynchronously and disproportionately on the particular areas that are most critical to your situation in the second half. It contains the practical nuts and bolts of applying these principles.

Before you get climbing, let's briefly review the trail map of what lies ahead.

Money: The first chapter addresses common misconceptions creative professionals have about profiting from their work. My goal here is to shatter the notion that focusing on the financial aspects of managing your practice might have a negative effect on your creativity. Financial success in creative entrepreneurship is not the result of "selling out." Your time and your work are valuable. The better off you are, financially, the more freedom and control you will have to do great work. And isn't doing great work the reason why you're getting into this business in the first place?

The corresponding money section, in the second half of the book, has two overarching goals. First, we're going to run through some basic math calculations so you can objectively see where your profitability problems are coming from, and how big those problems might be. This may be painful, but sometimes you need to face these realities in order to commit to change.

Secondly, it lays out some basic blocking and tackling practices for managing your practice, using standard financial reports and instruments. There may be a significant amount of work for you to do to implement changes—like getting into a real accounting system if you don't already have one.

Minutes: Time is a limited resource. How you manage it will greatly impact your practice. Similar to money, the practical implementation of time tracking practices will be found in the second half of the book, after you've gotten your head around the big picture.

However, I would suggest that, at a minimum, you begin tracking *all your time* starting now (including the time you spend reading this book). You don't need to think through all the categories and structures of a timekeeping system at first, but knowing how much overall time you're spending on your business is important data to collect. (By the way, if you are tracking this time, it should go under the category "professional development," but we'll get into those details later.)

Marketing: This chapter will require the most thought and boldest action. It will also require the most time to implement. I'm going to push you to make some hard choices in this section. So I don't recommend jumping straight there. Let your money and your minutes have their say first. Let them inform your goals and your plans. You'll need courage to take the necessary steps to effectively market your practice. But no doubt you're going to need to process this chapter, and evaluate these matters for some time.

When we revisit marketing in the second half of the book, I will guide you through some of the most difficult decisions any creative professional has to make.

Management: You might be wondering what the subject of management is doing in a book for freelancers. Aren't management principles for larger practices, with multiple employees? Not at all! Freelancers need management skills too since they have to wear a lot of hats. And so you're going to need to learn how to manage yourself as you fill each of the distinct "roles" that all creatives service practices must fill—whether there's just one or one hundred employees.

In this chapter, you'll learn that some roles are best fulfilled by individuals with specific kinds of work-style profiles. Yet certain profiles that are well suited for one kind of role may be completely unsuited for others. And there are even some work-styles and temperaments that are unsuited, or at least create serious barriers, for the primary role of running a business at all, freelance or otherwise. Your work-style can also indicate how certain work environments, work situations, or interpersonal work relationships may either motivate or demotivate you. These roles and responsibilities will always be in tension with each other. Yet, as a freelancer, you have to fulfill them all.

And so you need to start with yourself. There are facets of running your business that you love and enjoy—that energize you. And there are parts that you probably hate, want to avoid, and that drain you. This is true of everyone, though exactly which parts that do that will depend on your temperament. So managing yourself in the various roles and functions of your business can be helped by understanding your own work-style.

Depending on your work-style, you'll need to honestly evaluate how your strengths and weaknesses will impact your ability (and willingness) to fulfill all these roles. I'll offer some suggestions for how you can most effectively wear each of the hats and divvy up the various tasks, roles, and functions in such a way that they won't interfere with each other, or drive you crazy.

Lastly, when you consider these management principles, you should consider your long-term goals and ambitions for your business. Do you intend to hire employees in the future? If so, would you want to still be involved in the day-to-day creative work? How you answer that crucial question can have significant implications on when, and who, you might hire in the future. It will also impact how you wear the various hats, even as an independent creative professional.

Motivation: I'll be weaving motivation material throughout the book, but as you absorb all these practices you may start to feel overwhelmed. So we'll review some of the key aspects of motivation that challenge artists in business. I'll try to leave you ready to attack your work, to engage in the toil of the day-to-day business management aspects of your practice so that you will reap all the rewards your talents deserve!

Well, it's time to start heading up the mountain. There's a lot of ground to cover, so let's start the hike with the first subject, *Money*.

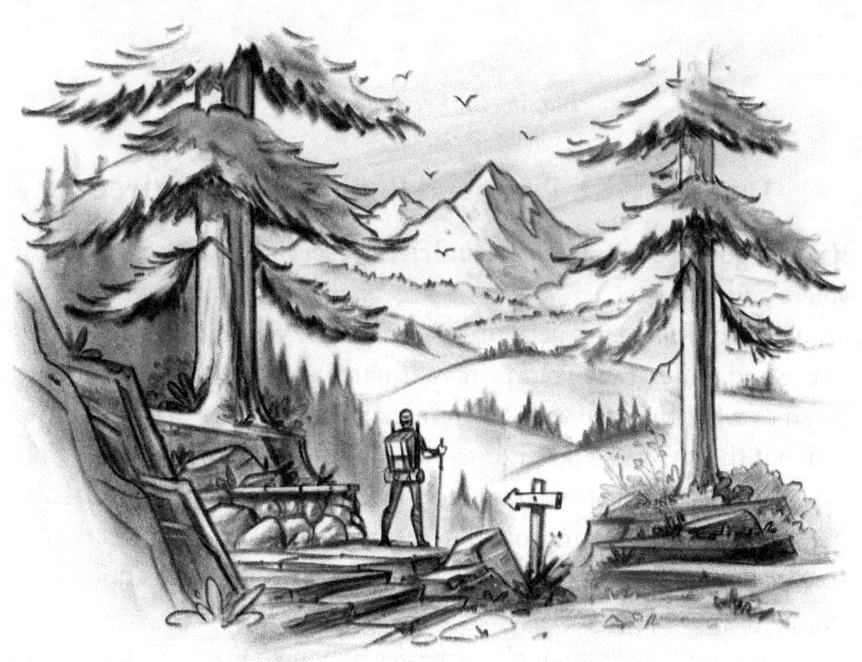

Chapter 1: MONEY

When my sister was eight years old, she decided it was time to become a reporter. We lived on Plainfield Street, so her newspaper was called, "The Plainfield Post." She sleuthed around the neighborhood collecting stories like "Dead Bird Found on Sidewalk," and "Mulligan Family to Sell Home." She typed up her stories, took a couple of Polaroids, and voilà, her first issue—a one-page broadside for sale, five cents each. Problem was, the library copy machine cost ten cents per copy. When my dad pointed out this disparity, she confidently responded, "Yeah, but I'm going to sell a lot of them!" Happily, my sister became more financially sophisticated when she grew up. But if you take an honest look at your business finances—if you calculate all your costs, all your expenses, all your overhead, and all your downtime—and using that data, calculate the effective hourly rate of your business, you might discover that your business plan looks as silly as the Plainfield Post's.

Dealing with Financial Realities is Required

If you're going to run a ***professional creative services practice***—that is, if you're going to run a creative practice *for very long*—you must become acquainted with the financial realities that drive your business. You need to use and understand your primary financial statements. You need to listen to what they tell you. Your financial statements may not flatter you, but they will also never lie to you.

Paying attention to your finances involves running monthly balance sheets, monthly profit and loss statements (P&Ls), and using a cash flow spreadsheet to predict the timing of your receivables in relation to the timing of your expenses.

Later, we'll walk through the basics of how to use and understand your financial instruments. It may take some time to gain these skills, to get your books in order, and keep up with them, but if you invest in this effort it will pay off with valuable insights into your business. We'll get into the nitty-gritty of QuickBooks® and spreadsheets later. For now, I think we need to address a more fundamental issue. It may be that you feel uncomfortable facing the financial aspects of your business, not due to lack of familiarity with financial instruments, but because of something deeper. You see, many artists resist dealing with money issues because they are conflicted, thinking that money and art shouldn't mix. Do you shudder at the thought of quitting out of Photoshop and opening up QuickBooks? There may be more at play than an aversion to dealing with minutia. You may be struggling with a fundamental inner conflict that forces an antithesis between money and the artistic endeavor. This inner conflict may have been imparted and deepened through experiences you may have had in art school.

Do you shudder at the thought of quitting out of Photoshop and opening up QuickBooks?

Chapter 1: MONEY

A Disdain of "Commercial" Art?

At some art schools, there is an unspoken hierarchy of the relative *prestige* and *purity* among its departments. The fine art department gets the highest regard, while the applied arts or commercial arts are sifted down to the bottom. Those in the painting and sculpting programs are most devoted to "Art" with a capital "A." In contrast, graphic design, industrial design, and illustration departments are not quite so pure. Now, of course, these tensions are all under the surface. Nobody would accept any outward expressions of such unflattering comparisons.

Nevertheless, this unspoken hierarchy exists. And many an art student has struggled with feelings of being a *"sellout"* when they decided to pursue commercial arts. And their creative consciences may have harshly accused them of artistic compromise.

What may account for this tension? I think it has to do with how closely commerce, money, and commercial interests intersect with the production of the art. There may be an underlying notion that the more money becomes a factor in artistic expression, the less pure are its artistic merits. And so, fine art is thought to be the purest form of artistic expression, because it's pursued for its own sake. The artist goes into the studio simply to paint, draw, or sculpt. How the work will be sold, if it will be sold, is a secondary concern. The sale of their artistic expressions *comes only after they've been produced*. On top of that, the artist has no first-hand involvement in the financial transaction of selling their work—the gallery owner deals with that. Therefore, its distance from money creates the illusion that pure artistic endeavor is untainted by money. Thus fine arts are subtly deemed to be a purer artistic product.

A commercial artist, on the other hand, whether a designer, photographer, or illustrator, must negotiate fees and sign contracts before applying their skills to a problem. Their product is more closely tied to money—and thus subtly considered tainted.

Such ideas are *nonsense*. Money, in and of itself, does not compromise artistic endeavor. Every artist requires income to provide for their lives and to continue their work. Both commercial artists and fine artists must engage in the business of art. Ignorant and unnecessary distinctions stemming from how money comes into the process only makes it harder for artists to manage their practices professionally. Artists have enough to struggle with when it comes to the business of art. Generally, most creative minds tend not to excel in data-driven tasks like bookkeeping and time management. And so dealing with the business and financial aspects of their work is difficult enough without having to bear the subconscious nagging guilt of being a "sellout."

Is Money Tainted?

So, in order to mute any lurking voices of condemnation from the conscience of the commercial artist, let's get back to some economic basics for a minute. It's said that money is the root of all evil. That's not true, and it's wrongly quoted. *Loving money* (*a.k.a.* greed) can, indeed, be the root of many evils (more accurately quoted), but money itself is not evil. In fact, money, as a financial instrument, is a *positive good*.

Money (or currency) is merely an instrument used to convey value. Having such an instrument is extremely helpful. Just imagine the alternative. Suppose you had to trade or barter for all the goods and services you needed. What if, every time you needed a gallon of milk or a muffler replacement, you had to locate a farmer or mechanic who also happened to need a new logo, or who liked your paintings? Money enables us to trade our goods and services to one party, and hold onto the value of that transaction for later use. Money allows us to buy and sell, trade, and acquire what we need at a fair and stable rate of exchange. We benefit tremendously every day simply because money exists.

Money is merely an instrument, a measure and conveyor of value. As such it's not evil; it's not even merely neutral; it is a good and beneficial instrument.

Is Profit Tainted?

And so, if money itself is not the problem, maybe it's the accumulation of money that bothers you? Maybe it's not money, but the idea of *profit*, that tweaks the creative conscience? No doubt there is such a thing as greed, and we don't want to be greedy. But does the fear of greed cause you to be uncomfortable with seeking profit from your work? Suppose you could set your fees at the top tier of your industry, and, as a result, gain far more than you needed for your basic living expenses. Would that bother you? Would you feel uncomfortable knowing that after completing each project you ended up gaining a 50% profit margin over all your labor and expenses? If you're uncomfortable with the idea of gaining profit, even substantial profit, from your work, we need to think that through as well.

Again, let's get back to basics and consider what profit is. Profit is simply the money left over after all the costs of labor, materials, and overhead have been paid out. Suppose, out of your discomfort with profit, you set your prices so that each project paid your costs including your personal compensation, but netted out to a zero balance. You covered all your costs, but with nothing left over. If you ran your business that way you'd be living in constant risk that if even one project ends with a deficit, you'd be left with debts—and if your prices are set to net out at zero, there'd be little hope that future projects would fill the hole. And frankly, it would be unfair for you to charge more to other clients simply to make up the deficit from shortfalls from others. Instead, you need to plan every project with a healthy profit margin.

All businesses must operate with the goal of retaining a profit on each transaction. All businesses build profit into their pricing structures in order to maintain economic stability. And the better your profit margin, *the more stable your company will be*, and the more control you will have over your work.

Profits Are Crucial for Freelancers

Profit margins not only reflect a basic economic need, but they also reflect the degree of risk a person takes in going into business for themselves. And freelancing can be a risky choice! There are no guarantees that you will have all the work you need next month. An employer will pay your salary even if they are light on work for a month. But as a freelancer, you enjoy no such regularity. And since you risk more, you ought to also reap more when you have success—and to create a buffer for the inevitable dry spell. Therefore, when you calculate your business costs, including your own compensation, you ought to assume a higher salary, and higher profit margin, than you might get if you took a more stable and dependable full-time position.

There is significant risk and stress that comes with being a freelancer. A steady paycheck and a balanced work schedule are two things you can count on never having. You'll never sustain having just the right amount of work. You will swing from having a bit too much work to not having quite enough. And sometimes those swings can be extreme! So you're going to need a healthy profit margin, and you're going to need to retain some of those profits, in order to even out the inevitable ups and downs.

Your profitability is a concrete measure of how valuable your talents are to your clients.

I hope that it's easy for you to see the need for a healthy profit margin. I don't think that's a hard sell. But is there a profit margin percentage that is too high for your comfort? If you were to increase a solid 15% to 25% profit margin (which is a minimum benchmark you should maintain) to a 50% to 100% profit margin—would you feel like you've crossed some ethical line? I don't believe you would have. You see, in a very important way, your profitability is concrete measure of how valuable your talents are to your clients, and to the marketplace. It is the most objective measure of how valuable your talent and your skills are compared to the availability of cheaper alternatives. Do you think your talent and your work have value? Do you feel like your creative services are below average? Average? Much better than average? To the extent that you're right about that, your profit margin is the measure that either proves or disproves that evaluation.

The Beauty of Economic Benefits

In order to put any residual art school inferiority complexes to rest, you need to make the shift from seeing profit as an indicator of greed, to a perspective that associates profit with the creation of new value. You see, business exchanges are not zero-sum transactions. An example of a zero-sum transaction would be theft. If you get mugged and have one hundred dollars taken from you, you've lost one hundred dollars and the thief gained it. Nothing is created in the process. Another example of a zero-sum transaction is taxes. When you pay your taxes you lose the amount you pay, and it gets redirected to some other end. No new financial value is created in that transaction. But when two parties engage in a business transaction, value is not just transferred, new value *is created!*

Think about it. When a client comes to you needing designs for their new product labels, before you do the work, those designs and labels do not exist in the world. The client has some money (that money exists), so they agree to pay you $10,000 to produce the designs. The designs (and labels) do not yet exist. You go to work and through your labor, your talents, your experience, your training, you bring something new into the world—you create a thing that did not exist—the newly designed labels. When you're done, something new exists in the world. They pay you, and yes, they have $10,000 less, and you have $10,000 more. The money still exists, it just moved from them to you. That transaction, by itself, is zero-sum. The world still contains that $10,000 (albeit in your bank account rather than theirs), but there is something new, too, something that did not exist prior to the exchange. You brought value into the world. And hopefully, they will take the valuable labels you've brought into existence, and use them to bring yet more new things, that do not yet exist, into the world—the products that will bear those beautifully designed labels.

You alone, through your labor, added value to the world, value that did not exist before you created it. Maybe I'm too easily pleased, but I find that to be a wonderful reality. When humans use their labor and talents to produce services and products, we bring new value into the world! People are value producers, not merely consumers. Artists are value producers, taking basic, simple materials, shaping them with their creativity—transforming paper and pixels into valuable works of art and visual communications.

People are value producers, not merely consumers. Artists are value producers, taking basic, simple materials, shaping them with their creativity—transforming paper and pixels into valuable works of art and visual communications.

But there is even more to gain in business exchanges. You see, every business transaction (provided they are entered into freely, fairly, and without deceit or coercion) not only results in new value, but as each party receives the benefits they contracted for, they are mutually improved. The client had money and needed design work. You needed money and had design skills. They wanted and needed your design more than they needed their money, and you were able to convert your skill, talent, and labor into the money you need for other things (like taking your friends out for dinner at that new bistro). Not only did a new thing, new value, enter into the world, but both parties benefited from the exchange, not to mention the benefit that the owner of the new bistro will soon enjoy.

Do you realize that every business transaction in which we engage, big or small, exhibits these wonderful traits? When you buy a pack of gum at the gas station, you get the gum and the station owner gets money. But also, more gum will be created to replace the supply you used, and so new value will enter into the world.

How Much Benefit? How Much Value?

In the case of gum, the value and benefit are fairly small, in part because gum is such a common commodity. But when something is rare, its value increases. Exceptional creative talent is a rare commodity. Your skills and talents offer great value. And this value is measured by your profit margin. Your profit margin is an objective measuring rod for the value you bring into the world.

I want to encourage you to start thinking about your profits, your bottom line, your *total equity* (a term defined later) as an indicator of the *value*, the *benefit*, the *good*, that you are bringing into the world through your talent and through your creative productivity.

So if you really think that design is valuable, if you really think that art is valuable, if you really think that your creative vision and skills are valuable, then you should expect, and insist, that this value produces its corresponding profit.

Rather than letting the commercial nature of your business diminish your artistic passion, you should allow money, and what it measures, to be the token of the value that you bring into the world. Money is not a stain on your creative effort; it is its reward—in more ways than one. So in the second half of the book, when we turn to the details of balance sheets, profit and loss statements, and cash flow spreadsheets, I hope that you will not just be gaining necessary skills, but I also hope these instruments will start to reveal the value that you create more concretely. So that when we see your total equity increasing, your heart will be warmed that your creative vision and artistic skill are producing measurable good in the world.

Establishing A Freelance Rate:
A Harbinger of Things to Come

There are a few decisions that any creative entrepreneur makes at the start of their career, that have far-reaching consequences. Establishing your rate is one of these crucial decisions. Later, when we dive into the details of managing money, we're going to run some calculations that will begin to show how important this number is going to be to the long-term health of your company. I've created a couple of online calculators (www.ericholter.com/resources) in case you're curious about some of those factors. But I don't want you to get hung up on the math right now. There are too many big picture considerations to address here, before diving into the details.

Determining an hourly rate is something every freelancer struggles with. Of course you want to capture as much revenue as possible, but you may also be afraid of pricing yourself out of an opportunity. And the self-cannibalizing habits of most of the freelance world creates a tight competitive environment that puts downward pressure on hourly rates. But it's a big mistake to set your rate too low. As you'll see, your profitability is going to be critical to your long-term health. If you don't make it high enough you may be shooting yourself in the foot. I'm going to push you to set a rate much higher than you're probably comfortable with.

Billing by the Hour Is a Losing Proposition

Most creatives start out charging by the hour because they lack confidence in their ability to accurately estimate the time it will take to complete projects. And so, billing by the hour feels safer. And that might be, sort of, at first. But consider a few realities. Your clients may accept your hourly rate, and accept hourly billing. But even so, they'll still ask you to estimate your hours for each project anyway. No one is going to write you a blank check. If you go over your estimate by very much, they might pay the overage, but they won't be happy, and they will question your competence. And since you know that's the case, and want to avoid that, you likely write off overages anyway—especially when you go way over your estimate. So your time estimate is going to function as a de facto project quote one way or the other. Under these conditions, *you can only lose.* If you go over your estimate, you lose because the client is not happy—or you write it off. If you go over but only bill the estimated amount, you lose revenue. Additionally, if you come in under your estimate, you lose out on the difference between your full estimate and what it actually took you to do the work. (Keep in mind if you negotiated to work for an hourly rate, and bill more than the hours you worked, that's fraud.) The only way you gain is if you happen to hit your estimate perfectly every time—and if you have confidence that you can do that, then you might as well quote the project in the first place.

When you bill by the hour, you end up getting punished for growing in your skill and efficiency.

Additionally, when you bill by the hour, you end up getting punished for growing in your skill and efficiency. The better you get at your job, the more competent and efficient you become through hard-earned experience, the fewer hours it will take to generate quality work—and under an hourly billing structure, as you get better you get paid less. Not a recipe for success.

On the other hand, if you quote by the project, you can be sure that you will capture that whole amount every time. It's true that you may lose if you underestimate, but you may also gain if you come in under the hours you planned. And, as you get better, faster, and more skilled, this will happen more often—deepening your profit margin in proportion to your growing expertise rather than shrinking it. That's a much better plan.

We'll talk more about how to produce accurate project quotes in the next section on "Minutes." But even when you stop billing by the hour, you're still going to need a benchmark rate to use in calculating your fees and evaluating performance. So let's consider some of the big picture factors that should go into establishing this crucial rate.

A Rate That Serves Your Future

If you run the calculators I referenced earlier, you'll see that when you take all the financial factors into consideration, a reasonably sustainable target rate is probably a lot higher than you thought. But there are other factors to consider besides expenses and downtime.

While this book is primarily intended as a guide for the freelance path, you may someday consider the possibility of hiring help. Before we examine that particular fork in the road, let's take a moment to consider that the rate you set today will impact your ability to make that decision if the time comes. A professional creative firm is expected to have higher rates than a freelancer. And it needs to in order to support the higher overhead. The moment you decide to hire your first employee, you take on overhead. And there are many costs associated with that transition that are rarely calculated. Will your freelance clients support a drastic increase in rate if that were to happen? Or would you suddenly need to find an entirely new set of clients prepared to pay higher rates or fees?

Freelancing is often the choice of the young. If your living expenses are relatively low, and you have only your own mouth to feed, you can afford to compete on price. But someday that might change. You might get married and start a family. You might want to buy a house. Your financial needs are almost certainly going to increase over the years. Don't build your practice on the low hanging fruit of clients that value you primarily for affordability.

We're going to return to these considerations in the chapters on Management, but for now, as you're setting down the important stakes of your rates and fees, take a look at the horizon and set yourself up for long-term success, don't undercut your future by selling yourself short.

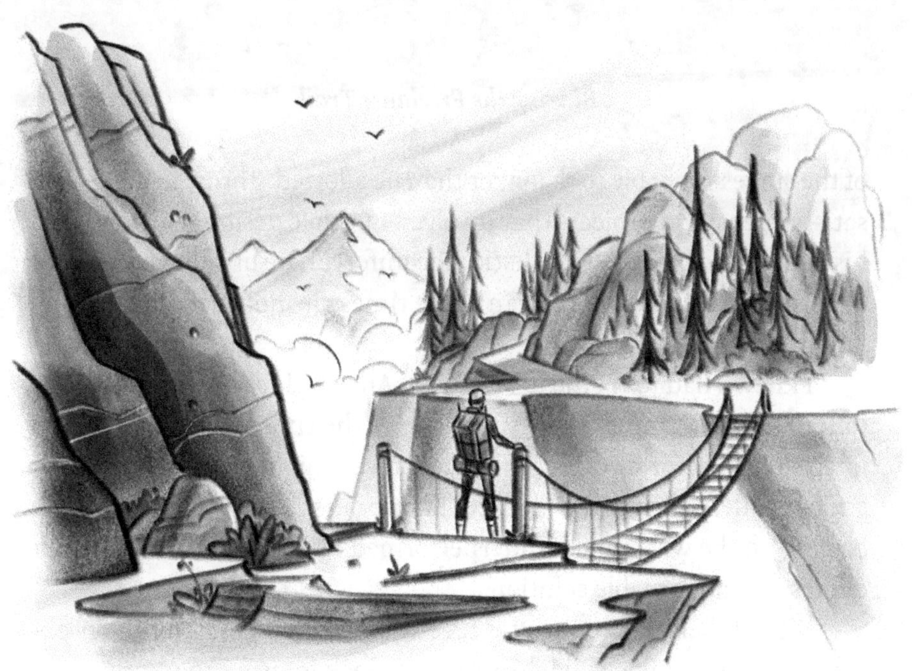

Chapter 2: MINUTES

In the early 2000s, when I was still just getting my first web development company off the ground, one of my project managers took it upon himself to put together a Gantt chart of one of our typical web development projects. He laid out all the stages, the specific tasks associated with each stage, and all the employees involved throughout the process. He carefully noted all the tasks that had dependencies. Working with all this data he developed a model project schedule that forecasted the total time each stage took, and their impact on an entire project. When he presented his research, he summarized by telling me that we had been spending at least *three times* as many hours on our projects than we had scheduled, and more depressingly, than we were getting paid for. My first impulse was that he had to be wrong.

But after I carefully scrutinized his results, I was forced to acknowledge that his evaluation was accurate. Worse, that in most cases his time estimates were on the conservative side. In any given real project, some of the stages probably took longer than he allotted. Throw in a hard-to-satisfy client, and projects that involved multiple design revisions, and his plan started looking idealistic. The unfortunate upshot was that we were spending even more than three times the hours than had been budgeted for our projects.

I knew I had to fix these problems. And the idea of charging three to four times as much wasn't realistic at the time. If you know your internet history, or if you lived through it, you might recall that the early 2000s are described as the "dot com bubble burst." Most companies were cooling on the web; it had underperformed expectations. Tripling our quotes was not a viable solution.

What I really had to do was fix our bloated process. But the problem was that I had no solid data to use to look for ways to improve. My project manager's efforts were based on hypotheticals, on interviewing employees, and following a few current projects in general. In order to go deeper, I needed actual time data, to see exactly where we were bleeding hours. But we had not been keeping timesheets, so I was out of luck. That data would have been golden to me at that moment. We did start keeping time records after that, but it takes many months, spanning multiple projects, before enough new time data can be collected and used for evaluation. You don't miss those records until you really need them.

I did end up fixing our process, and we survived the bubble burst. But that was probably the result of chance, as well as being blessed with a couple of big, key opportunities that enabled us to shift, survive, and even thrive after the market turned around. But playing games of chance is not a good way to manage your business.

Managing a Business Means Making Decisions

Running a business, including a freelance business, involves making many decisions. Sales decisions, marketing decisions, scheduling decisions, quotes and estimates, and more. Unfortunately, when it comes to making these kinds of decisions, we make them blindly. We don't have any hard data to guide our decision-making process. So we guess. And when we guess blindly, we're usually wrong.

Measuring Every Minute

Let's cut to the chase. You need to start tracking your time—all of it. If you charge by the hour you have to track your time in order to invoice your projects. But if you don't measure *all your time*, every minute, including the time you spend on administrative tasks, sales and marketing time, even professional development—unless you're measuring all the time you spend at work, you will not have the information you need when making important business decisions.

Unless you measure all your time, every minute . . . you will not have the information you need when making important business decisions.

Time tracking, and time evaluation, are fundamental disciplines every business owner needs to practice.

Why is time tracking so neglected? Let's step back and consider some of the reasons artists and designers don't track time—other than, perhaps, their project time (aside from the obvious reason that timesheets are a pain in the neck). There may be some deeper reasons why creatives, like yourself, object so strongly to time tracking.

Common Objections to Keeping Timesheets

"Deadlines Kill Creativity"

The most common creative objection to tracking time is that "deadlines stifle creativity." Artists and designers resist time pressures insisting that "the creative process can't be rushed." We've all felt the discomfort of trying to perform under time pressure. Taking the SAT was stressful, not just because of the importance of our scores, but because we had to race through the tests, dreading the looming command of "all pencils down."

Granted, artists and designers can't do their best work if their managers are incessantly standing by their desks, tapping their feet, looking at their watches, and asking for status updates. Too much of that kind of pressure will, indeed, affect the quality of their work. But, of course, we all know that projects have limited budgets—we can never have all the time we want. Time is an absolutely firm, nonrenewable resource. We can't make more of it, so we have to carefully portion it out. And though we may complain about budgets and deadlines, we still have to work within schedules, and conform to design budgets, albeit sometimes begrudgingly.

When creatives balk at keeping time sheets, I think it's because it takes that stifling necessity of sticking to a budget, and brings those constraining deadlines forward hour-by-hour as they work. It's one thing to know that there is a looming deadline, and overall time limit to a project. It's an altogether different thing to be reminded of that reality every time you stop and start work. And so the mere act of jotting down your hours or entering them into a time-tracking system may constantly reinforce your awareness of the limits of time. And since artists don't like limits, the act of time tracking may cause them to feel like their process is constantly being impinged. Therefore, my advice that you start tracking *all your time* may provoke a negative response.

How can you come to grips with these tensions so that you can capture the valuable resource of time data, without stifling your creativity? I think there are some ways, but it may require that you start thinking about time limits in new ways.

Be More Like Leonardo

In days past, artists were craftsmen. Today they are more like explorers. In days past, becoming an artist involved long, arduous apprenticeships with a master—repeating the same tasks, sharpening core skills, and mastering one style. Today designers are inundated with all manner of experimental techniques and endless options of media, typography, and formats. When I studied typography in the late eighties, we still had to draw letterforms by hand, and specify typography with mono-spaced manuscripts marked up for photographic typesetting. And my particular interest was handset metal type. So when composing a broadside or book layout, I had three or four font sizes to work with, if I was lucky. I'm glad for this experience because I can relate to what Leonardo da Vinci said about the real source of creativity, "Art lives from constraints and dies from freedom."

Can we as modern creatives learn from the wisdom of the ages? I think we can, but if we do, we'll need to rethink how we relate to the tensions of time on our creative efforts.

Overcoming Resistance to Time Tracking: Have a Long-Term Outlook

Bill Gates once quipped, "Most people overestimate what they can do in one year and underestimate what they can do in ten years." Applying this to artistic endeavor, it may be that our intense desire to perfect the immediate project in front of us may blind us to how our artistic vision, skill, and maturity are going to be cultivated *over the years*. I think, as designers, we always want every project to be a masterpiece. Do you ever think to yourself, as you are working on a piece, "Maybe this will win an award," or, "How good will this look in my portfolio?" This ambition for the immediate project can create an insatiable appetite for more and more time to perfect the piece. This is an example of overestimating what we can accomplish in a year, or with just one project.

But what if, instead, we took the long view? What if we focused on how each project contributes to our lifelong creative experience? What if we increased our appreciation for how every new problem is slowly developing our creative point of view? What if, instead of swinging for the fences every time, we just committed ourselves to putting out good work time after time, week after week, not getting caught up in the eddies of the stream of perfection? What if we learn to integrate the limitations on our time into the mix of the elements that define the creative process, so that those limits *add to the creative challenge* rather than diminish the creative product?

Maybe, if we can make these mental value shifts, we can start to view time as an ally, rather than fighting it as an enemy. Then, instead of striving against the clock—a striving that undermines our efforts (and our budgets), we can learn to give what we can under the time resources available for each project, and consider each opportunity one more step toward building our creative expertise over the long haul.

We need to come to terms with the relentless clock if we're going to free our creativity from the boundaries and realities of limited time.

We need to come to terms with the relentless clock if we're going to free our creativity from the boundaries and realities of limited time. We need to get comfortable with time constraints. Otherwise the simple, frequent, mechanical act of logging time—the starting and stopping of timers—will remain a continual tension. After all, clicking a digital timer doesn't take much time, but failing to reconcile tensions with time may cause those few seconds to feel disproportionately weighty, reminding us all day long that time is running out. We can't let the simple three-second act of clicking a timer provoke anxieties about deadlines and budgets. So let's take the long view and let time limitations serve the creative process.

This tip helps resolve the negative barriers pertaining to time tracking, but let's consider a more positive rationale for time tracking that will benefit the creative process.

Measuring Time's Benefit to the Creative Process

In addition to coping with the psychological pressures of time tracking, you can also make peace with the clock, and your timesheets, by understanding how the effort of collecting time data benefits you. Sure, collecting time data is a pain, and yes it may remind you of impending deadlines, but the goal of measuring time is to enable you to make better estimates and schedules based on real data. Without this time data, you can only make educated guesses about estimates, schedules, and budgets. And bad guesses inevitably result in poorly budgeted and scheduled projects which will cause far more anxiety than whatever minor tensions you might feel when you log your time. Bad guesses create serious time pressures, and many other discouraging realities that stem from a lack of profitability—and those pressures really will hurt your business and impact your creativity.

But, as you will see, engaging in the simple daily discipline of recording your time will create a valuable resource, collecting the necessary information—the only information—that will help solve more consequential problems that create real stress. After all, a properly budgeted (though still limited) schedule will enable you to do the best work possible under the conditions available. But an unrealistically limited schedule and budget, resulting from poor insight and lack of information—will, indeed, diminish your creative efforts.

So, in addition to overcoming the tensions inherent in day-to-day timekeeping by taking the long view, we can overcome our momentary reluctance to measuring and reporting time by remembering that these bits of data are contributing to a valuable, irreplaceable resource, that will work to your advantage. You're helping yourself when you keep careful track of your time.

We need to make time our ally in the design process instead of striving against a reality that, sooner or later, wins out anyway. When you do have consistent, complete, and accurate time information you will have a valuable data source for evaluating performance, improving processes, and measuring efficiency.

Making Use of Your Time Data

Collecting complete and accurate time data creates a valuable resource. But in order to realize that value, you have to know how to use this information. There are two main ways that your time data will be used: producing accurate quotes and schedules, and evaluating performance.

Producing Quotes and Schedules

The most basic use of your time data is establishing future pricing, quotes, and project schedules. When you evaluate your time usage, you will become more accurate in gauging the effort needed to complete future projects. And as you build a deep well of historic data, you will be able to see exactly how much time it takes you to complete various assignments. That information will keep you from seriously underestimating future projects—and preserve you from making costly mistakes. The historic data will also quantify some of the time expenditures that we tend to overlook when estimating. We tend to forget all the phone calls, meetings, and administrative tasks that every project entails. Only by reviewing past projects will you properly forecast future budgets.

Using your time data for estimating future allocations is aided tremendously when you establish consistent project categories *and phases*. Not every project is the same. But certain phases of a project may have commonalities that can be used for estimating new projects. For example, maybe you produced a brochure for a past client that is similar in scope to what a new client needs. But the original project required a completely new visual concept. This new project will rely on the client's established branding standards. If you only had project totals for the old brochure project, that data would not be an accurate source for estimating the new one. But if you broke up your design and concept phases from the production and prepress phases, you could still use the old project as a guide for estimating similar phases.

In addition to preparing better quotes, solid historical data will help you to establish better project schedules. Projects typically take longer than we think, especially when we hit roadblocks. Sometimes project roadblocks might be of our own making, but more often than not they come from the client's side. Timely feedback and approvals are often hindered when feedback needs to filter through a client's internal layers of management. These known but unpredictable slowdowns can really disrupt our schedules. And without real data to remind us, we tend to forget these specific instances when putting together new schedules. But if we look at historic examples, where time and time again a schedule expanded beyond its original allocation, we'll learn to build in flexibility. Seeing the overall timeline of past projects will give us a basis for being more conservative in committing to deadlines or promising delivery dates that may be unrealistic.

Being Your Own Project Manager

Each of the five main subjects that structure this book: Money, Minutes, Marketing, Management, and Motivation all interrelate. And Minutes and Management are particularly connected, so I need to preview a bit of the Management topic here as it relates to managing minutes.

One of the overarching tasks of a project manager's role is to bring a project in on time and on budget. Accomplishing this goal for projects with extended timelines, multiple resources, and external clients is no easy task. It takes specialized skill, abundant communication, and lots of diligence to be a good project manager. Various professional roles are most suitable to individuals with work-styles that match them. And generally speaking, the creative professional does not have a work-style that's well suited to project management. Additionally, the nature of the creative process requires a good deal of sustained and focused work. It's not easy to switch back and forth between creativity and responding to urgent communications. In larger firms, the roles of creative and of project management are separated and handled by professionals suited to each kind of work.

But for the creative freelancer, working solo, all these functions have to be handled by one and the same person. To make matters more complicated, in a creative firm, tasks can be shuffled between various resources when projects stop, restart, and overlap. They have a bit more flexibility to adapt to adjusting and overlapping schedules. But for the solo freelancer, you will have to adjust to uneven project flows. The project management task is, therefore, more difficult since its resources are less fluid. Yet, creative temperaments and the creative process both make functioning in this role more difficult.

We're going to come back to this complicated subject later. I'm forecasting this problem to underscore how important it is to be recording *all your time* to build a data source which will become one of your most valuable assets for managing yourself and your practice in the months and years to come.

What Your Time Will Tell You

Once you start looking at your finances regularly, and measuring and evaluating your minutes, you're likely to discover, as I did, that the numbers don't look so good. You can make some gains by plugging holes, adapting your process, and looking for efficiencies. But the real problems with your profitability, that your money and your minutes will tell you, is that you are probably not charging enough for your work. Improving your profitability is most likely going to require charging more for your work. Otherwise, the only two other options are to eventually go out of business, or burn out from subsidizing your clients with your unpaid labor.

But this solution, to charge more, is easier said than done. And transitioning to higher rates and bigger quotes won't happen overnight. Ultimately, you're going to have to find clients that are willing to pay your higher rates and accept larger fees. And finding such clients is going to require a *radical upgrade to your marketing*.

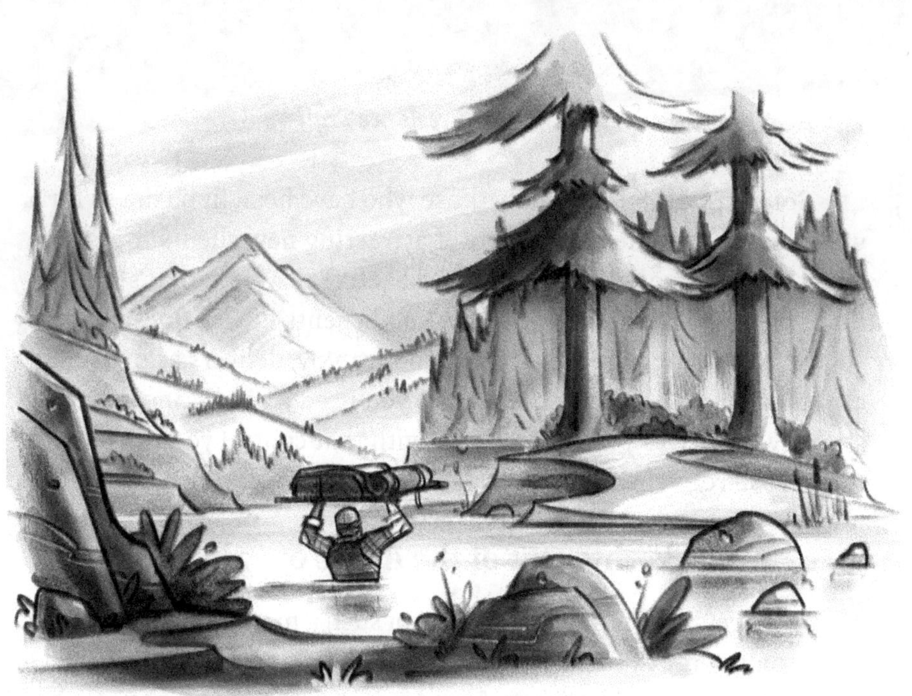

Chapter 3: MARKETING

Welcome to the heart of this book. In some ways this really ought to be the first chapter. But there's a good reason why it's in the middle of the five "Ms" that structure it. I'm going to call upon you to make some difficult, maybe even scary, decisions. I think, when you've had time to thoroughly process this chapter, you will see why it's so important. I put the matters of Money and Minutes first, because until you listen carefully to what they have to say, you might not have the wherewithal to face the solution in this chapter. But once you see that many of the problems you may be feeling can be traced back to profitability challenges—and if you want to fix those—you're probably going to need to start charging more for your work. While some of your existing clients may accept new, higher rates and fees, those will probably be the exceptions. That means you're going to have to find new clients that are willing to pay more for your work. And that is the goal of marketing—upgrading and *controlling* the quality of your client base.

Some creatives, especially those who have been in business for a while, may have a decent history of attracting new clients. But these clients come through reputation and referral. While that's fine, as far as it goes, and can deliver some good clients, it also does not give you control over client acquisition, and frankly, delivers as many bad clients to your doors as good. And so you need a marketing plan and strategy that gives you control, and with that control you can set out to improve your client base.

Marketing Out of the Ashes of Failure

Before we get into the specific aspects of such a marketing plan, let me share some of my experiences with marketing my design firms. When I was running my first company, I tried just about everything to get new business. I sent letters out to local companies. I made beautiful, direct-mail, letterpress broadsides. I ran ads in our local business newspaper. I hired PR to get us press. I sponsored public radio. I bought banner ads and ran AdWord campaigns. I attended local business trade shows and attended networking events. I produced videos. And, at one point, I even bribed prospects to give us an opportunity to make a capabilities presentation by offering to bring a chocolate cake! I tried every marketing approach I could think of, and none of them generated much business.

Putting in that kind of effort, with so little to show for it, is discouraging to say the least. Maybe you've experienced the same? But my experience in marketing changed. I did find a way to cultivate regular new business opportunities. And you can learn to apply the same principles to improve your marketing efforts. Let's begin by making sure we're operating with a common understanding of what marketing really is. We need to start by clarifying a couple of key terms.

What is "Sales" and What is "Marketing?"

There is an important distinction between *sales* and *marketing*. To sum up the difference, "marketing" consists of all the efforts you make in order to get your phone to ring, or to get an email form filled out. "Sales" is really a subset of marketing. It consists of the things you do and say *after* your marketing efforts result in an *opportunity*. Sales is the process of persuading a prospect to hire you, once your marketing efforts have paid off, having brought an opportunity to your door.

When your marketing is working, sales is the easiest part of the process. When you've been passive in marketing, sales can sometimes be a nightmare. You've probably experienced some easy sales processes, particularly when a prospect calls, and there's a perfect fit between their needs and your abilities, availability, and affordability. Other times you may feel like you're having to work extremely hard to overcome objections and resistance to your fees. Good marketing should result in well-qualified prospects approaching you with appropriate opportunities that match your skills and who can afford your prices. When these things align, sales is simple. When they are out of whack, things don't go so well.

I'll come back, toward the end of this chapter, and describe how solid marketing makes sales a snap, but for now let's take a closer look at what effective marketing efforts look like.

The Key to Marketing: Narrow Positioning

After years of fruitless marketing efforts, I finally learned how to get results. I discovered a way to find prospects, and dependably turn them into good clients. So much so, that by the time I sold my first company, we were having to do very little outbound marketing. Instead, we had a consistent stream of qualified inbound leads. Our sales efforts began to consist more of deciding between opportunities, which ones to accept given the limits of our capacity (and which ones to decline), than it did trying to convince prospects to hire us.

The Bitter Pill of Narrow Positioning

But here's where it gets difficult. Solving your marketing problems will require something that "artistic ambition" shrinks at. It's called *narrow positioning*. Effective marketing depends on narrow positioning. It requires you to set limits on the kind of work you will do, and for whom you will do it. Narrow positioning requires that you be able to precisely define <u>what you do</u>, <u>for whom you do it</u>, and <u>how it benefits them</u>. These three questions must be answered, with as much precision and clarity as possible, if you are going to gain leverage in your marketing.

Solving your marketing problems will require something that "artistic ambition" shrinks at. It's called narrow positioning.

Most designers, however, based on their websites, do the exact opposite. They define what they do as broadly as possible. Their capabilities lists include anything and everything they've ever done: websites, online marketing, advertising, logos, brochures, packaging, video, outdoor. Additionally, they list as many market sectors they've worked within as possible: healthcare, technology, education, packaging, financial services. And how exactly does their work benefit the client? To summarize their pitch, "because, branding!"

This is the polar opposite of narrow positioning—it is wide-net positioning. It's desperate positioning. And prospects can easily sniff out desperation, and then leverage it to their advantage.

Adopting a narrow position is the only way for you to get control of your marketing, and to improve your client base. But here's what I know from experience. Even if I persuade you of this claim, you will probably not want to do it. There are some deep-seated reasons why you, as an artist, may resist this idea and hope that there can be some other way. So before we walk through how narrow positioning works, and why it's indispensable for effective marketing, we need to diagnose more fully the fears and tensions that might be rising up inside your heart from the very suggestion that you need to limit the kind of work you seek.

Positioning and the Artist's Dilemma

Artists have a hard time with positioning. We don't like to narrow our focus, do we? We like to explore! We don't want to repeat the same kinds of projects over and over again. We want to play! We don't want to master one thing. We want to try many new things. As a result, artists are rarely willing to take this important first step toward effective marketing.

If you haven't read David Brooks's best seller *Bobos in Paradise*, you may want to put it on your list. He does a masterful job of demonstrating how social and psychological tensions between our bohemian impulses and values and our more bourgeois instincts impact our engagement with culture. His application is broad, but his insights are profoundly applicable to the artist's temperament. You see, the creative heart is bohemian. It wants to try new things, experiment, explore. But the *business* of design is more bourgeois. It's settled, focused, committed, and mature. I think this tension between the bohemian and bourgeois runs deep in the commercial artist's heart. And it sits at the core of why so many creatives fail in business.

Practical Benefits of Narrow Positioning

The braver and bolder you take hold of this concept, the more your marketing efforts will result in easier sales, and better, more profitable clients and projects. Here are some practical ways that a narrowly focused position will get you there.

1. Locating Your Market: If you had to build a list of potential contacts to reach out to right now, before adopting a narrow focus, where would you begin? In fact, go to LinkedIn right now and open the advanced search page. What search parameters would you use to identify a list of potential new clients? Are there any limits? Geography, perhaps.

But wouldn't you be willing to work for a qualified client, with a great budget, even if they happened to be located across the country? For the typical creative, without a narrow focus, the search parameters for listing prospects includes just about anyone. So long as they need some design work, and have a reasonable budget, they qualify. Your LinkedIn parameters are effectively "all" in every category! You can't know where to begin.

2. Speaking to Your Market: So with "all" as your search criteria, let's select any company or contact from the list. With that particular prospect in mind, what would you write or say if you were going to make a cold call or send an unsolicited email? You see, without a defined market, you have no place to start—and nothing persuasive to say.

Without defining your position in the market, you can't even begin to find your market. On the other hand, if you narrowed your search parameters based on the second positioning statement question, "who you do it for," you'll have a place to start. Consider this example: Let's take "poster design" as our "what we do," and "for art galleries" as our "who we do it for." Now, it's easy to narrow a LinkedIn search to art galleries. And there are many other criteria that might influence your list. Perhaps you only work for fine-art galleries, and perhaps you look for galleries with five or more employees (big enough to afford your fees).

Now consider what you might say to them in an email.

> "Hello _______, my name is _______. I am a graphic designer who specializes in poster design for high-end art galleries, to help them promote their upcoming exhibits. I believe that the marketing materials used to promote your talented artists should be treated with the same high standards as the work itself.
>
> I've produced marketing materials for _______, _______, and _______. I'd love an opportunity to speak with you about

how my work can complement and extend the reach of the artists you will be representing in upcoming exhibits."

Now, of course, such an email won't generate a reply every time, but it sure can surface leads more effectively than a generic email—or more likely, no email at all.

3. Persuading a Prospect: The last part of the marketing puzzle, that narrow positioning benefits, is the sales opportunity itself, the occasion to persuade a prospect to hire you. Once you find a prospect, you need to convince them that you are able to deliver, and that your fees are worth it. You do this through a website that demonstrates your experience and expertise in this area. The example above would show posters used to market fine-arts exhibits (and little else). And if it also included blog posts or articles on subjects related to designing posters for art exhibits, all the better. As your expertise grows you'll become aware of the challenges and opportunities gallery owners face. Your insights might become greater than theirs since they only have their own experience to go by, while you will have helped dozens of galleries.

Now before you start freaking out at the prospect of limiting your artistic focus to just one kind of work, and even further, constraining that to just one industry or client type, let me offer an important clarification that might temper your anxiety a bit. And I'll also share a few advantages that can emerge from narrow positioning that you should consider which may actually increase your *creative and artistic output* (even as it improves your marketing efforts).

What Narrow Positioning Does Not Mean

Narrow positioning will apply to your *active marketing efforts*. Your focus will help you go after new clients and new work. But it does not define what work you ultimately accept. Nor does it require that you fire all your existing clients that do not fit into this new focus. If a client from a different industry comes to you, you're perfectly free to accept that work. Narrow positioning commits you to not *actively seek variety* in your marketing not that you never accept variety.

Creative Advantages to Narrow Positioning

Narrowing your focus may seem scary, and it will be hard. But consider some of its creative advantages.

1. Creative Air: Remember the big picture. Narrow positioning is necessary in order to improve your client base. You need better clients that can afford to pay you what you're worth. Narrow positioning is necessary, ultimately, to increase your *profitability*. Now there is no doubt that operating unprofitably puts serious downward pressure on your creative expression. Being behind schedule, worrying about cash flow, being desperate for new business, operating over budget, all these symptoms of unprofitability will quash the creative process. So while narrow positioning may reduce the range of your creative expression, it will improve the operating conditions under which you work, which will significantly improve the quality of your creativity.

2. Shoehorning Creativity or Having Freedom to Perform: Creatives sometimes take on clients or projects that they know are not a great fit, or whose budget is too low, on the premise that it will provide a creative opportunity. The odds of that panning out are short. I worked for two award winning advertising agencies in my early days. And while they sometimes won awards for their main clients, the majority of their award-winning creative work was for their pro bono clients. Paying clients play it safe. You can count on your paying clients to pick the least creative solution you present, to the consternation of many a copywriter and art director. But when the ad agency offers their high-caliber creative team to a local cause, for free, they get greater creative freedom—beggars can't be choosers.

So if you are ever tempted to take on a paying client, even if it is a low-paying client, because of the illusion of creative opportunity, think again. The most creative ideas you bring will often get shot down. You may end up spending extra time on already low paying projects, in pursuit of a potential One Show entry, and end up shelving the brilliant concepts for the safe one that the client chooses. On the other hand, if you build your practice on solid, well-paid-for expertise, you will have profits that free you to offer true pro bono services to whomever suits your fancy, and get real opportunities for creative freedom.

3. Professional Development: The higher profits that arise from narrow positioning can be spent in other ways that benefit creativity. With profitability also comes increasingly available free time. If you become profitable, you could reserve seasons for creating for the pure enjoyment and exploration of new ideas. So rather than looking for client opportunities to scratch your creative itch, you could use your professional development time for unrestrained creative exploration. If you do become profitable, why not consider taking a few weeks off for creative vacations?

4. Craftsmanship: Lastly, consider the vast historic precedent for how artistic exceptionalism has come about, not from expansive exploration, but through the artistic legacy of *craftsmanship*. The greatest artists in history became great because they honed and mastered their craft day after day, year after year. Early on, in my artistic career, I found myself drawn to the Arts and Crafts movement, to artisans like William Morris and Eric Gill. (Not surprisingly my degree project was in letterpress printing, wood engraving, and fine-press, handmade books.) These kinds of artistic disciplines required a great deal of focus, practice, and cultivation of skills (you'd be surprised what goes into effectively sharpening an engraving burin).

When a designer or artist adopts narrow positioning they can redirect their bohemian artistic identity into a craftsman, or artisan, identity. We can acknowledge that the greatest forms of artistic expression have come from doing the same thing, again and again, until we have become masters of our craft.

When a designer or artist adopts narrow positioning they can redirect their bohemian artistic identity into a craftsman, or artisan identity.

Have the world's greatest masters, ever complained that they were bored in their work? No, on the contrary, they grew more fascinated the deeper they delved into their disciplines.

Take an evening to watch the Netflix documentary *Jiro Dreams of Sushi*. It's about an aged Japanese man who has spent his entire life making sushi. His small restaurant seats fewer than a dozen people, but the waiting list to experience his masterful creations is extremely long. If you were to get an apprenticeship there, you would spend the first few years learning how to prepare the rice, before you'd ever be allowed anywhere near a fish. Or check out *Crafted*, by Morgan Spurlock, on Amazon Prime. It follows the stories of a handful of artisans who have focused on doing just one thing well. The results of their rigor produce outstanding and sought after creations. You may need some inspiration like this to help you unlock the artistic pursuit of craftsmanship, in order to undergird your courage for honing a narrow positioning.

It may be a challenge to contemplate reining in your creative focus, but I'm going to ask you to do just that.

A Sales Illustration of Marketing
with a Narrow Positioning

If you are able to focus your talents in a concerted direction, you will not only find marketing easier, and more productive, but the sales *experience* will also become more enjoyable. Let's compare two hypothetical sales experiences, one that results from passive, generalist marketing, and the other from marketing with a narrow positioning.

The Sales Experience of the Passive Generalist Position

Most creative firms, lacking a focused expertise, have to rely on referrals and their reputation for leads. Not only is such marketing harder to control, but also each individual sales process is harder to manage for the generalist. Consider the dynamics of a typical sales moment for a generalist.

Having received a lead, you schedule an initial call or meeting. Since this lead came through a referral they could be any kind of company with a wide range of needs. And so, right away, you have a lot of work to do just to get a basic understanding of their needs. What does this company do? How big is it? How long have they been in business? How many locations do they have? What is their position in their market, and how are they trying to grow or change? What is the nature of the project they need help with? What are their needs and expectations for turnaround time? Who is the intended audience? What results are they expecting? Who would the main contact be? Who are the decision makers? And the mother of all intake questions—what is the budget for the project? And so the majority of your time, during this initial conversation, where you make that all-important first impression, has to be occupied with getting loads of basic information from them—and vice versa.

All these particulars and more need to be unearthed during that initial contact. And while you're in the process of collecting that information, you have to begin accessing some of the subjective aspects of forming a relationship with this prospect. Would they be a good fit for you? Will they treat you like a professional or like a vendor? Under such condensed and complex sales conditions, it's difficult to make sound assessments.

Then, of course, they have questions for you. But since you don't really know this prospect well, or what their real needs are, you'll probably find yourself responding with generalities. And if you happen to be desperate for new work, you might make unrealistic promises or exaggerate your capabilities.

Whew. Those can be some intense and difficult new business conversations. But then, after the conversation, the ball is in your court to send a proposal. With only rudimentary details, your proposal will have to major on boilerplate information about your experience, vision, and creativity—and minor on your assessment of client's needs. And your estimate page will have to reflect your gut feeling of their budget, rather than any meaningful analysis of the project's requirements.

But you write it up, send it off, and then you wait. Maybe a few days later you place a follow-up call—and leave a message. Maybe a week later you email them for a status and again wait for a reply. Maybe you do end up winning the project. Or maybe you never hear anything back at all—or perhaps you are at least given the dignity of the curt, "We've decided to go in a different direction" reply.

Contrast: The Sales Experience of the Narrowly Positioned Expert

Now consider that same initial call, but from the perspective of a creative practice that has carved out a narrow position and collected meaningful experiences in that one area of expertise. For the sake of this example, let's assume your expertise is designing printed recruitment materials for private secondary schools.

The first contrast to note is, unlike the passive marketing of the generalist, you don't have to wait around for your phone to ring or an email to arrive. You know exactly how to find your prospects. Just go to LinkedIn and search the Primary/Secondary Education industry and filter by the function of principal or marketing director. Then send an email—you can reach out along the same lines as the art gallery poster designer example. Since these messages are meaningful to your prospects, and tailored to their specific needs, targeted prospects may very well click through to your site. Even a cursory review of your content and portfolio will demonstrate to them that you have deep experience that clearly matches their needs. If they dig deeper and read a few blog posts that speak to their needs, they'll be even more reassured that you're someone they need to talk to. Some specialists, being confident about what it takes to solve the kinds of problems their clients face, are able and willing to go so far as to list benchmark prices on their websites. Such transparency reinforces their confidence in your capabilities, and helps clear the budget hurdle before a conversation even begins. In contrast to the generalist sales process, which can be an uphill battle, for the specialist, prospects arrive half sold.

And so by the time you have that first call or meeting, many of the questions that a generalist has to ask are already known. You already know that they are a private secondary school. You already have a good idea of the issues they face. You already have a handle on how most secondary schools are organized, and so you can ask deeper questions about the relationships between their board of directors and their administration. You have familiarity with how the politics of such organizations can affect project schedules. And you already know what their budgets are (or need to be).

Unlike the varied tensions that accompany an initial sales meeting for a generalist, when the specialist talks with people whose problems they fully understand, the conversation itself is a hopeful experience for the prospect.

Consider a medical analogy. Imagine if you moved to a new area and suddenly developed some concerning and debilitating symptoms. Before you can get help, you'd need to find a general practitioner (which can be challenging enough these days!). That doctor would have to spend most of your first appointment asking you all about your medical history, family history, overall lifestyle, including details down to your daily vitamins. But you want to know why you're suddenly so sick you can barely work! After an hour of forms and intake procedures, in the end all they can do is refer you to a specialist (hopefully the right one, but often that process is a journey of its own—I hope you've never had to take it). But imagine, if after months of trying to find help you meet a specialist who looks at your chart and is able to quickly diagnose and confirm your problem, and provide a solution. As a patient you will leave that appointment so much happier than the one you had with your general practitioner! And when we find that relief, we gladly pay their higher fees.

Calls between a specialist and a prospective client who needs that specialization are quite affirming. As you share your experience and expertise with real, clear answers to their needs, they feel like they're breathing fresh air. How many times have they had to prod and poke potential new designers, sifting through vague and generalized answers to questions looking for some substance? They get tired of the dance as much as creatives do. And they're as afraid of making bad decisions (and being held responsible for the outcomes) as you are of not getting their business. How refreshing for them to find a designer that really does know their world! Instead of rolling the dice on hiring a generalist, finding a specialist gives a prospect a strong sense of confidence that their needs will be met.

Finding a specialist gives a prospect a strong sense of confidence.

Once that initial call is over, and it's time to write a proposal, you already have a number of past proposals that form a robust starting point. You just have to tailor one for this particular opportunity—one that contains more substance over boilerplate.

Finally, after you've been awarded the business, and you deliver a product that highly satisfies your client (and when you get paid!) your creative confidence will grow all the more! Repeated positive experiences like this will transform the dread you might now feel facing new business development, into confident anticipation of new opportunities to practice your craft—to the benefit of your client and to your continued success.

This kind of positioning is challenging (but not impossible) to get started. But once it's in motion, it gains its own momentum, and gets easier and easier over time. As you grow in your area of expertise, your work will improve, and your experience will produce insights that will further bolster your brand and persuade yet more prospects.

Are There Any Alternatives?

I've done my best to persuade you that narrow positioning is key. It stands in sharp contrast to the typical generalist positioning of the average creative practice. Once this key principle is explained, most artists and designers understand why it's so important, and see its value. But most are also resistant to making this kind of limiting choice.

Maybe you're unconvinced, or perhaps too reluctant to choose one main thing, limiting yourself to one industry and specializing in one area of service. Maybe you're still in the early launch stages of your career and your rocket boosters are still filled with the fuel of artistic passion. Frankly, it does take many years of running on the generalist freelance treadmill before enough fatigue sets in to motivate creatives to make serious changes. But I still have a hope and a vision for a generation of young creatives who can see far enough out ahead that they start their professional careers heading in the right direction with the necessary tools and equipment, so that they don't have to learn through painful failure, or near death exhaustion before taking the business side of their profession more seriously.

But if you're not there yet, keep reading. There are still many aspects of the management principles in this book, which, if properly instituted and practiced, will certainly improve your business. Listening to your money, tracking your time, managing your roles, and having some kind of marketing plan certainly can't hurt.

But can a generalist thrive? Yes, it is possible, and I want to give you at least some idea of what it would take to succeed as a generalist—even though I do not recommend that path.

Let's review the limitations of a generalist positioning compared to a specialist positioning, and then consider some ways you might compensate in order to survive and perhaps thrive as a generalist.

Limitations of Generalist Positioning

1. Price Competition. As a generalist, your rates and fees are going to be tied to the standard rates of your competitors. If your talent level, or experience, or reputation is significantly stronger than a competitor's, you may be able to get away with slightly higher fees, but not by much. The perceptions of your talent, experience, and reputation are in the eye of the beholder. And if there are plenty of alternatives for work, any significant disparity in prices between your services and your competitors will be hard to justify. Specialists, on the other hand, can charge more because their expertise is rare. The laws of supply and demand act on your rates and fees just as they do on a commodities market.

2. Lack of Control in Marketing. One of the most crippling limitations for the generalist is the lack of control over marketing. Casting a wide net as a generalist is not only hard to do, but you never know what you're going to pull up. It might be a beautiful marlin or an old tire. You'll also have to work harder and see fewer results from those efforts. That's why most generalists end up subsisting on new business from reputation and referral, which is great when work is flowing, but it's terrifying and unfixable when things slow down. A specialist, on the other hand, knows where to find their market and they always bring a compelling pitch to those prospects.

3. Expansive and Inconsistent Processes. When you regularly gain clients from many different industries, with a variety of needs, you will always be behind the eight ball when it comes to learning how best to solve their problems. They may need solutions that you don't regularly provide. And so you'll need to research and educate yourself on new processes, procedures, and products. The startup who needs a new logo may hit your sweet spot, but when they ask for trade show graphics and the production of swag for a conference, you may have to do a lot of research on everything from suppliers, to lead time schedules, to new formatting requirements. All this may be interesting, but it is also inefficient.

4. High Overhead in Client Acquisition and Orientation. When you sit down with a prospect whose business is in a sector you're not familiar with, you will have a much longer list of diagnostic questions to determine their needs. Additionally, when it comes to writing a proposal, you'll either submit boilerplate information about your practice with a best-guess estimate, or you'll need to invest considerable time doing research, investigation, and preliminary strategy for free. The overhead of educating yourself about each new client's business can be quite high.

Who Can Thrive Under Generalist Conditions?

There are a lot of limitations and liabilities to maintaining a generalist position. But some creatives are able to make it work, at least for awhile. So if you want to continue down this path, and have some hope for success, you should soberly consider some things about yourself to help determine if this is a viable and sustainable option. Creatives can thrive as generalists if they are . . .

1. Frugal. Creatives that can sustain a generalist position will need to have modest needs, and relatively low expectations for compensation. If you are, by nature, a frugal person, then you may be able to sustain a generalist practice.

2. Extroverted. If you're an extrovert, who gets energized by meeting new people, and doing a lot of networking, and making new relationships, then you may be able to survive as a generalist.

3. A Fast Learner. If you're going to thrive as a generalist, you'll need to be a fast learner, able to intuitively and quickly adapt basic marketing and design principles to broad, generalized problems. If you're smart and quick on your feet, you can shorten your learning curve when acquiring clients with varied needs in new industries.

4. Short-Term Employers. A generalist may thrive if they are not hesitant to hire (and let go of) short-term help, on an as needed basis. Workflow will never be steady, and so if you can bring on an intern, or contractor, and then have no problem releasing them when the work slows down, you may be able to thrive as a generalist.

5. Highly Efficient. To thrive as a generalist you need maximum efficiency. You will need to develop efficient processes and keep a close eye on your project's statuses at all times, rigorously sticking to budgets. If you can stop working when the solution is good, without pressing in for greatness every time, you may be able to make a generalist practice work.

6. Young. If you have many of the traits listed here, *and you're young,* you may be able to make a go of a generalist practice. Generalists need high energy as they scramble to find work, maintain their competitive edge, and cope with lower rates and fees. Many young designers have these traits, but begin to lose them as they get older, get married, have kids, and outside time demands and financial needs increase. For these reasons I don't recommend this path, even for the young, because it's not sustainable in the long run. And it's hard to shift gears later when your client base expects low cost as a part of your offering.

Trade-offs for the Generalist Practice

If you're going to stick with a generalist position, you should understand some of the trade-offs you're making in this choice.

1. Impact for Expansive Opportunities. As a generalist you will never be viewed as a strong strategic partner. You will be viewed as a vendor, not as a business advisor for marketing and design. But that's okay—the world needs competent design vendors. And so if you own this trade-off, and structure yourself as a highly competent and efficient vendor, you will be more successful than if you're always getting frustrated when your clients order you to make the logo bigger.

2. Strategy for Aesthetics. Creative professionals like to talk about the strategic importance of branding. And there are important elements to brand strategy. But not every design project demands a rebrand. Sometimes businesses and organizations just need their materials to look good. And so if you don't try to oversell, and instead focus on delivering nicely designed, aesthetically pleasing materials, on time and on budget, you can become a valued vendor, who gets lots of repeat business, and leave the deeper strategy to others.

3. Quality for Quantity. Since your profit margins will always face downward pressure from competition, you won't be able to afford much downtime. So you're going to need to stay busy. Therefore clients that have needs for more frequent, smaller projects, may be more lucrative for you than big ones with occasional large projects.

There are many generalist creative practices—in fact most of them are. But it's also true that most creative practices don't last very long. So if you're in this career for the long-term, then my advice is to leave the generalist position to the young and inexperienced. And instead, up your professional profile and become a focused expert. In the long run, this is the soundest, most sustainable and rewarding path.

Can You Endure Narrow Positioning?

I know that narrow positioning is a hard sell to a creative soul. I hope the notion of cultivating an artisan or craftsman's approach might help you to make a bold and brave decision. I hope the idea of controlling your marketing and continually upgrading your client list are also strong motivations.

Keep in mind that just because you will be choosing to only go after one kind of work within one main business segment, that does not restrict you from accepting other kinds of work that may come your way. It only restricts the kind of work you deliberately seek out. It also does not restrict you from exploring creative ideas and applications in your professional development—or in your free time—free time afforded to you by your profitability.

The only alternative is to passively wait for work to come your way, or pour out your effort in general marketing with meager results.

I'd encourage you to give this serious thought, and to begin to bolster your courage to move toward narrow positioning. When we return to this subject we will work through some exercises that are designed to test your positioning and help you craft an actionable and effective marketing position.

Bolster your courage to move toward narrow positioning.

After listening to your Money, and measuring your Minutes, and making hard Marketing choices—you'll need to start thinking more about the next "M"—you'll need to think more about Management practices. Whereas creative firms need to manage employees, if you want to remain a freelancer, you will have to manage your growth. And that presents challenges and difficulties of its own.

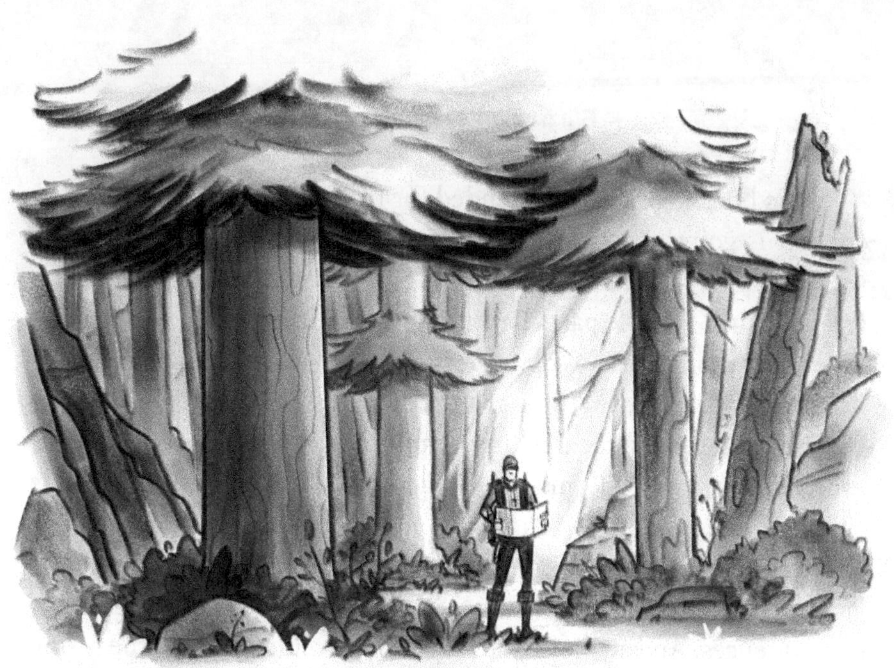

Chapter 4: MANAGEMENT

The first three principles demonstrated how the frustrations and struggles that freelance creatives face in business result from the core problem of *unprofitability*. And so the focus and goal of the last three chapters were to identify the issues that cause unprofitability, and turn things around. This chapter, on Management, is going to anticipate your success, and start to address some new problems that will arise as your marketing efforts begin to pay off, and you regularly have more opportunities than you can accept. When that happens, you're going to come to a crossroads, and you're going to have to choose a path.

Once you've successfully established your marketing, and have plenty of profitable work to choose from, you're going to have to address the problem of what to do with all the work you can't take on. Successful marketing will lead to many opportunities and you won't be able to accept them all. And so, you'll come to the big fork in the road where you have to decide whether or not you should *hire help*.

This book is primarily intended for freelancers so the bulk of this chapter is going to assume that you will decide to continue down a solo freelance path, and not hire help. You should know that long-term freelancing is a viable path. You can respond to growth *without hiring*. You can be profitable as a solo practitioner (and in contrast, many larger design firms are miserably unprofitable).

Nevertheless, since the hiring option will always be a possibility, especially when you become successful, I want to take some time in this chapter to address important issues you will need to consider, should you decide to explore the hiring path. Failure to anticipate this particular crossroad is common to most creative practices, and can lead to extreme consequences. And so first a warning: don't ever head down the hiring path without carefully considering the ramifications of your choice. Hiring should be the result of careful and thoughtful planning, not a knee-jerk reaction to a spike in demand for your services.

The progression from successful freelancing to building a growing firm is typical and normal. But it is also fraught with failures and mistakes. There are good reasons to grow from freelance to firm, but there are a whole host of bad reasons, too. If you decide to hire, this book is insufficient to prepare you for that path. Before you involve the livelihoods of others in your business choices, you may need more hands-on consulting and evaluation.

After exploring the hiring path a bit, we'll return to the issues of applying management principles to your freelance practice.

Two Common Mistakes When Heading Down the Hiring Path

Let's consider two ways that creatives end up heading down the hiring path, and some of the mistakes they make along the way. First, we'll consider the mistake of hiring simply because you're overworked and stressed out. And then we'll look at the mistake of hiring in reaction to a spike in demand rather than as a deliberate, reflective, and well-considered choice.

Hiring to Avoid Burnout

As a freelancer, you wear a lot of hats. You have to find work, do the work, bill the work, and maintain your business as a whole. It's a careful balancing act, juggling all your different roles and responsibilities. And since your volume of work is never steady, you end up alternating between scrambling for new work and then, when you're busy, trying to complete it, all the while responding to unexpected requests from existing clients that show up at just the wrong time. Managing your own workflow under such conditions is a big job in and of itself. As you get busier it may seem like the administrative aspects of your job are eating up so much of your time that there's little left for creativity. You may find yourself spending more time on the phone, sending emails, and going to meetings than you spend being creative. You may find that the only time you have for production is pushed off to nights and weekends. That's not a sustainable lifestyle. And when you've been burning the candle at both ends, when you finally do get down to creating, fatigue prevents you from doing your best work.

Reactive hiring only compounds your problems.

It's circumstances like these that drive a freelancer to start looking for an escape hatch. You just want to create. After all, you went to art school, not business management school! And so you come to the crossroads where there seems to be no other choice but to hire help.

Hiring under these circumstances is called *reactive hiring*. And reactive hiring only compounds your problems, especially when you're busy, with lots of work, not even realizing that the work itself is not profitable. Let's try to quantify the compounding problems you may face if you hire reactively. Let's assume that, as a freelancer operating under the conditions described here, you are not hitting your financial benchmarks. For example, your overall *utilization* is less than 60% (we'll dive deeper into some of these benchmark terms and calculations in chapter 9), and your *effective hourly rate* is therefore lower than you realize. You are, in effect, selling ten cent newspapers for a nickel. What do you think the outcome will be if, under those circumstances, you add more overhead to your business by hiring help?

Let's apply another mathematical model to see how hiring because you're overloaded with unprofitable work compounds troubles. Let's try to calculate the *loss of efficiency* that comes from hiring new staff. Adding a new staff member never increases your productivity level by a whole person, especially not right away. First, there's the training time: orientation, gaining familiarity with clients, and learning processes and procedures. Training time will eat into the productivity of your new hire. Then there are additional subjective aspects that eat into productivity. There will always be interpersonal learning curves involved in forming new working relationships. Work-styles, expectations, relative strengths and weaknesses (and how they interact), as well as our basic personalities and temperaments will need time to gel. Let's assume that at least initially, for the first month or two, there will be a 50% efficiency loss with every new hire.

But that's not all. You have to take your own productivity lag into account. After all, you will have to take time away from other activities in order to train this person, walk them through their assignments, and simply interact with another person in your day-to-day work life.

So while hiring a new employee will add an entire new salary to your expenses, you will only gain an initial 35%–40% production capacity from that hire. That's a pretty big hit. But there's even more to consider in terms of efficiency. Eventually, this new hire will get past the training phase, they'll learn the ropes and become efficient. But they will never be 100% productive, every staff member will carry some overhead. At most you can expect between 80%–90% productivity from a production employee.

And even at peak efficiency, you will have to spend some of your own time managing this employee, so even after you've invested a significant percentage of your time training the employees, managing them in the long-term will consume at least 10%–15% of your own efficiency.

In order to sustain your business over this training period, your work is going to need to have a significant profit margin built into it. But even a basic 15%–20% profit margin will be strained under these conditions, so you should have about a month or two of the new hire's salary saved up in order to smooth out this transition. In the scenario we're running, we're assuming that one of the main motivators for hiring is desperation from overwork *because of unprofitability*. So you see, reactive hiring can lead to many more problems than you may have had in the first place.

Mistakes from Hiring from Success

But maybe you are profitable, and have cash reserves, and plenty of opportunities, having established a solid footing in your marketing, and so you decide to hire from your success. That is a much better basis, but there is another potential mistake you might make even under sound financial conditions.

Let's change the conditions from the previous example, and assume that as a successful freelancer, who is hitting all your financial benchmarks, and who has profits and savings, you decide to grow your practice and hire help. The key mistake creatives make under these conditions is in deciding who your first hire will be. Will you hire another creative to help with the work itself? Or should you hire an account manager to help you deal with client communications that are eating into your design time? Or should you hire a salesperson to handle new business? These are all perfectly reasonable options to consider. But the key mistake you might make in deciding who to hire first is not determining what *your long-term role will be* in this new firm. Who you hire first, and what roles you seek to fill by hiring, will start to shape the *kind of firm that you will become*. And your own role in that firm will be shaped by how you go about hiring.

In some regards, making the choice to go down the hiring path at all is going to require you to function more like a business owner than as a creative. Adding staff, at a minimum, will add human resources matters to your to-do list. And even if you eventually hire managers, as *an owner* you will have to manage the managers. So the hiring path will fundamentally change your job from being a creative doer, to owning a creative company. Managing managers, making hiring decisions, and giving creative direction will all become new requirements added to your role. How much these new responsibilities will take over your creative work is something you need to think carefully about from the beginning. Do you intend to transform entirely from a creative to someone who owns a creative business (who no longer engages in the creative product at all)? Or do you want to continue to create? *This is a huge consideration!* If you do not answer this for yourself, and instead hire willy nilly, by default you will end up spending all your time managing the company, no longer doing the work. And if this was not your intention, and you end up resenting your new responsibilities, you will probably not manage your business very well, and you'll be constantly frustrated.

This is why, if you are hiring because you are successful, you will immediately come to another fork in that road, requiring you to decide what your long-term role in your company will be. If you are not intentional, and plan accordingly, your transition will be frustrating and painful, and probably lead you to places you never wanted to go. And once you've hired, correcting course could require letting employees go. So please, I reiterate again, seek professional assessment and advice before heading down this path.

The Big "Step" of Hiring Your First Employee

I want to add another financial warning before you head down the hiring path, particularly with respect to the *first* employee—regardless of whether this is from reactive hiring or planned hiring. You need to consider the disproportionate effects of *stepped costs*, when it comes to hiring your first employee (in contrast to adding a sixth or seventh). The smaller your firm (and when you hire your first employee, it's as small as it can be) the more you will feel the effects of the stepped costs of hiring. You see, there will be a huge step up in your overhead costs, going from one to two people. You double the number of salaries. And yet your sales volume is not likely to be ready for such an immediate increase.

When creative entrepreneurs start to feel the strain from being overworked, thus leading to reactive hiring, they are not likely to have been operating at 200% capacity (which would fully justify adding a whole new salary to match the work on hand). Once a person nears 150% capacity, they're more than ready to seek help through hiring. Yet, while having so much work that you're at 150% capacity is a serious problem. That workload is not sufficient to cover a 100% increase in staff compensation. And so while your overhead will double, your sales volume will lag. You'll go from one person working at 150% to two people at 75% capacity (with respect to sales volume), but it won't feel this way. Given the efficiency hits described above, you will probably both feel like you're working at 100% capacity. And yet, your bottom line will not reflect this. Hiring one person has doubled your staff, but also immediately halved your sales volume. This will have a predictably unfavorable impact on your profitability. So in the midst of the pressures of training the new employee and managing significant efficiency drops (putting even more pressure on your time), you now also need to focus more time on your marketing efforts in order to get your sales volume up to supply the increased overhead (further impinging your overall productivity). The stepped costs of hiring this first employee are steep!

In contrast, while stepped costs are experienced by larger firms too, the proportions are more manageable. Consider how adding a tenth employee only increases staff overhead by 10%, and requires only a 10% increase in sales volume to cover. That smaller step can be comfortably covered by even a modest profit margin on existing work.

A Final Test Before Hiring

If you do, after considering all the liabilities associated with hiring, decide to head down this path, you should ask yourself an important "gut check" question. If you make a mistake in hiring, is it in you to fire someone? This is a critical question (and also a good reason to avoid hiring your friends). You will almost certainly make mistakes in hiring. Can you bring yourself to fire someone who is incompetent, or perhaps ill-suited for their role (even if the reason they are ill-suited is because you messed up by hiring them for it in the first place)? Under whatever circumstances, if an employee is not working out, can you fire them? If you cannot say yes to that question, *you should not hire employees*. Failure to fix employee problems and fix hiring mistakes, in a timely manner, will run any company into the ground. No doubt firing someone is a difficult and unpleasant experience. But if you can't do it, don't head down this path.

So your first hire is by far the most risky and will have the greatest financial impact on your practice. Making your first hire without first attaining a healthy profit margin (and setting some of those profits aside to cover the transition) is a recipe for disaster. Reactive hiring is a bad idea, by all counts.

No 50/50 Partnerships!

One final mistake needs to be addressed, which many creative entrepreneurs make when considering whether or not to hire help. And that is to form a partnership with a friend. It's a familiar story: two colleagues contemplating starting a new firm, but lacking the confidence to do it alone, join together. Whatever hesitations they may have had individually get bolstered and reassured by their mutual willingness to enter into this adventure together. And so it's off to the races. Of course, all the complicated paperwork, and legalese involved in forming the partnership, or LLC, is the last thing on their minds. So they dash off a cheap 50%–50% LLC so they can get on with all the fun stuff, like designing the firm's identity and website.

Unfortunately, it's easy technically, to enter into a business partnership or form a basic LLC. But it is harder, and messier, to *get out of one*. Failure rates for partnerships in general are high (statistics vary, but greater than 50% is conservative). And those that make up most of the 50% of successful partnerships are impersonal real estate partnerships, or law firms who have long-standing and well-known partnership structures. Those who enter into design firm partnerships usually do not understand the implications of this decision. And so when they fail, which they usually do, the personal and emotional consequences can be devastating.

So please think twice, or thrice, or as many times as necessary until you conclude that *you should not enter into a partnership* (or 50%–50% LLC). Because they almost never work!

There are other alternatives for two or more parties to go into business together without forming a partnership. For example, one party can employ the other and offer profit sharing. Or you could form an LLC and give a smaller amount of ownership and restricted voting rights to one of the parties, based on their role and intended long-term contribution. But please, if you start looking down the hiring or partnership road, make sure you're doing it for the right reasons and with clear business aims and goals.

Staying Small and Profitable
by Learning to Say "No"

It's time to get back to that initial fork in the road and consider the option this book is designed to help you with, the decision to stay on the freelance path and not hire help. So what do you do when your marketing is bearing fruit, and you have more opportunities than you can say "yes" to? What are the alternatives to hiring?

Successful marketing results in a steady stream of qualified leads who all want to work with you. The result of successful marketing should enable you to choose from among many qualified potential clients and pick just the best ones. That sounds nice, doesn't it? Except when it comes to turning down a real-life client, saying "no" can be extremely difficult. If we find it difficult to say "no" even when a potential client's budget is too low, imagine how hard it will be to say "no" to a perfectly qualified prospect with an adequate budget.

Successful marketing results in a steady stream of qualified leads.

How hard will it be when such a prospect really wants to work with you, but since your time is limited, and you happen to have a couple other opportunities that are a bit better, you have to decline? Disappointing people is never easy. But unless you can do that, then success is going to be hard for you to bear. Yet that's the goal! To always have more demand for your work than supply. Under such circumstances you can become very profitable. You can increase your fees in proportion to increased demand. But the corollary to that successful scenario is that you will inevitably have to turn work down. You won't be able to take on every opportunity, not even every qualified opportunity. And so you will have to say "no."

One way to get better at saying "no" is to start with those opportunities that are not qualified to begin with. Designers get in trouble because they take on projects whose budgets they know are not sufficient. They justify taking the job anyway by granting nonprofit discounts, or a family and friends rate. Now, if you are profitable, and consciously decide to volunteer for someone, or subsidize a client out of genuine altruism or charity, that's fine. But if you do not have that kind of freedom from existing profitability, then you are giving something you don't have. And it will cost you. So start getting used to saying "no" by rejecting those projects that you ought to be saying "no" to anyways, as practice for the day when you'll have to say "no" simply because you've chosen to be a successful freelancer.

Wearing All the Hats

Saying "no" when you have more demand than capacity is your first line of defense as your marketing gains traction. Another way that you can address this challenge is by maximizing your own efficiency so that you can say "yes" to as many opportunities as possible. That means you'll need to be an effective manager of yourself, as you fill the various roles of running your practice. When we circle back around to this subject in the second half of the book I'll provide more detail on the specifics of managing yourself.

But let's at least outline what some of these roles are, and how as a freelancer you will occupy them. There are four main roles to consider: the production role, administrative role, the client service role, and the marketing and new business role.

The Production Role. The production role is the core of what you do. This is the role that comes naturally to you. The main change you may face in occupying it in the future is managing your productivity within the constraints that come from filling the other roles properly. This will inevitably limit the time you have for creative production, and require you to engage in tasks less suitable and less attractive to your inclinations. But you should already be comfortable in this role.

The Administrative Role. The administrative role is definitely one that stands in tension with the creative spirit. It's the role that reviews how you're spending and allocating your minutes. It's the role that has to listen to what your money is truly saying and make hard calls. And it's probably your most neglected role. Transitioning from free-range freelancing into running a well-managed creative practice will initially require large doses of administrative change.

The Client Service Role. As a freelancer you probably have a knack for client service. I don't think a solo creative entrepreneur would last long without at least some gifting in client relationships. But since you are both the producer of work and the deliverer you face some unique dynamics that can lead to dangerous distortions when you function in the client service role. But if you can learn how to integrate administrative functions you should be able to compensate and improve your client services.

The Marketing and New Business Role. Most generalist creative practices neglect this role. They rely on having one cornerstone client, or on relationships and referrals. And frankly, with a generalist position, marketing efforts are so low-impact that it doesn't make sense to spend extra time marketing. But with narrow positioning you will find that proactive marketing is an essential element to long-term stability, sustainability, and profitability. You're going to need to make some time for putting on the marketing hat.

As a solo creative entrepreneur you will have to occupy each of these roles at various times. That's a lot of hats to wear. And not all of them will feel as comfortable as the others.

For now, you just need to recognize that if you're going to be a good boss and leader to yourself you're going to have to do what all competent bosses must do—hold your employees accountable for their work and performance. You don't have to be great at all of these roles, in fact you can't be. But you do have to perform them all, and hold yourself accountable.

A Lot to Take In

Congratulations, we've covered a lot of ground. We're nearing the summit. You may want to take a rest there, put down the book and think about what it really means to engage in a creative startup and run it like a professional business.

But before you take that breather there is one last "M," the "M" of Motivation. And you're going to need some of that as you consider many of the ideas we've covered, and anticipate the hard work of implementing changes as you blaze your new path down the other side.

The next chapter will be a little different. There won't be any new tactical concepts. But I hope that it will inspire you, and help you to reflect on your reasons for doing what you love to do as an artist and that it might even purify and strengthen those motives so that all your toil will result in many rewards.

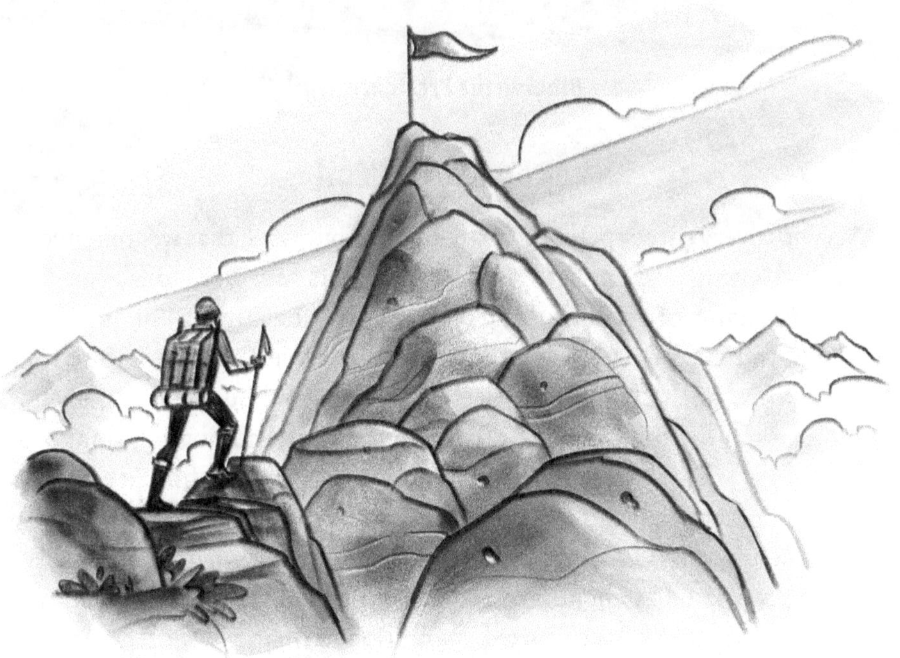

Chapter 5: MOTIVATION

Being a creative entrepreneur is hard work. The disciplines of art and design are demanding. And the disciplines of business are likewise challenging. The complexities that arise from the combination of the two, especially for the artist, are part of the reason why so many freelance practices fall short of success.

This book focuses on concrete business skills that designers and artists need to master in order to build profitable and sustainable creative practices. There are many business management tasks that fall under the headings of Money, Minutes, Marketing, and Management that creative professionals need to get a grip on if they are going to make it as an independent freelancer. Having laid some foundational concepts and as you prepare to work through the concrete tasks and efforts to implement changes, now is a good time to stop and reflect on what it means to be a creative professional. We need to address our fundamental motivations and draw attention to some of the challenges that are deeply ingrained in the creative drive.

Rewarding Toil

As with every career path, there are parts of our work that we find inherently exciting and engaging. And other parts are, well, toilsome. The original name of my consulting practice was "Rewarding Toil" because I've found that artists and designers who are able to embrace the parts of their work that they don't prefer, the toilsome business tasks, end up reaping the most rewards from their work. And not just financial rewards—the most well-run, well-managed, and profitable creative service practices generally produce the best creative work. And doing good work, providing real value, delivering quality that is recognized and appreciated by clients and improves the lives of others, can become a deeply soul-satisfying reward in addition to financial success. And so my goal as a professional mentor to creative entrepreneurs is to help you cultivate not just higher profit margins, and find better clients, but to help you discover an even deeper satisfaction in your work.

This chapter will be a bit different from the previous four. There won't be much in the way of learning new concepts, or systems, or tasks. Instead, I want to put some fuel in your tank, and to encourage you as you contemplate all the effort that will be needed to improve your practice, and to help you to stick with your plans. These are the *ends* for which I want to motivate you. But you need to know that the *means* by which I'll motivate you might be surprising.

A Higher Goal to Aim For

Up until this point we've focused on concepts that are necessary to make your practice *profitable*. That's a good goal. But as we all know, financial success does not always bring happiness. Sometimes money brings misery—just ask the average lottery winner. I hope that these principles will make you profitable. But even more, I hope that they make you *happier* in your work. And so while my basic goals are to improve your profits, I want to press further in and help you increase your happiness in your work.

It is always my assumption, when dealing with motivation, that all artists—all humans for that matter—ultimately desire the same thing from their work that they do from the rest of their lives. We all aim for *happiness*. The pursuit of joy, or happiness, or satisfaction, or pleasure in all of life, including our work lives, is fundamental to human experience.

If you don't identify with this assumption and assertion—if I'm way off base in your case—then you can skip this chapter. But if I have a bead on your deepest desires for being a creative professional, then read on.

Deconstructing Artistic Motivation

We're going to take a circuitous route in this chapter as we address motivation. Before I can build you up and motivate you toward greater joy and happiness in your work, I need to deconstruct some other motives common to the creative enterprise that tend to get in the way, and distract, or can even counteract the experience of joy in artistic endeavor.

We need to put our finger on some of the other, deep, motivations that reside in the artist's heart. And we may need to adjust, perhaps uproot, or at least change the trajectory of some of these motives, in order to move toward greater joy and happiness in your work.

The Complicated Connection Between Work and Meaning

What gets you up out of bed in the morning? What fuels your day? Besides coffee I mean. What keeps you going day after day, week after week, year after year? Obviously there are the necessities: we work for food, clothing, and to pay our rent. But the necessities of life are not the only thing that motivate you, right? You probably want more out of your work than a paycheck (and if that's not true you probably picked the wrong career!). Artists and designers want their work to be interesting; we want it to be successful; we want it to be satisfying. In a word, we want it to be *meaningful*.

I'm going to come back to this underlying goal, for our work to be meaningful, in a moment. But since the interrelationship between work and meaning is deep waters, we're going to need to dissect this claim in more detail. But let me state upfront the reason why diving deep into this topic is necessary. I'll be arguing that *striving for meaning—particularly when we seek meaning in and through our work—introduces distortions and diversions from our ultimate goal of finding happiness.* If you would kindly grant me that premise for now, I'll try to support it more later. But if it's true that a rigid insistence on doing work that both reveals meaning and is meaningful can undermine happiness, then I would suggest that creatives driven by artistic passion are *more vulnerable* to unhappiness in their work than other professionals. Why might that be the case?

> *Creatives driven by artistic passion are more vulnerable to unhappiness.*

The Artist's Unique Relationship to Work

The artist's relationship to their work is complicated. All people tend to identify with their chosen professions. When we meet new people, we exchange our names, and the next question is usually about what we do for a living. While we all identify closely with our work, creative professionals identify themselves *as artists*, in their souls, more deeply than most. They put more of themselves, more of their heart, more of their identity into their work than is typical of other professions.

One way to observe this deeper connection between artists and their work is to contrast it with other professionals. Compare, for example, the average design firm website with that of any other small professional services business. If you read the average accountant's, or lawyer's, or carpenter's website, you will find that the bulk of the content focuses on their work *product*. They almost never emphasize their own personal values, or their love for doing the kind of work they do, or their experiences in doing their work. Art and design websites, on the other hand, often feature a personal love for creativity itself, and belief in the goodness of art and design. They feature their aesthetic values and the culture of the artist or firm. Sometimes there can be as much, if not more, emphasis on the culture, values, and aesthetics of the workers than on the work itself! This contrast points out how artists relate to their work, not merely as a product or service to be offered to a market, but as something more, something deeper, *something more meaningful.*

Creatives *are* artists. Accountants *produce* tax returns.

And so, if my initial premise—that striving for meaning in our work can distract from happiness—if this premise is true, and if it's also true that creatives are more connected to their work than most—then creatives, in particular, are in great danger of unhappiness, and more vulnerable to short-circuiting joy in their work, even as they so passionately engage in the creative process.

The Connection Between Meaning and Work

I think, if you are a creative professional, you know by experience that your work is more deeply connected to your identity than it is for other professionals. And so, if there is this danger in seeking too much meaning and identity from our work, then artists are more susceptible to this danger than others. Just as a coal miner is more susceptible to black lung disease than an airline pilot would be, the drive for meaning in work is a greater occupational hazard for the artist than for the airline pilot!

But is it true that our pursuit of happiness, in general, tends to find expression in the pursuit of meaning in our work? I believe that it is, but let me qualify this assertion a little before I try to further prove that this is the case.

I take the pursuit of happiness as a given. The seventeenth-century philosopher Blaise Pascal also asserted this as a given.

> *"All men seek happiness. This is without exception. Whatever different means they employ, they all tend to this end. The cause of some going to war, and of others avoiding it, is the same desire in both, attended with different views. The will never takes the least*

> *step but to this object. This is the motive of every action of every man, even of those who hang themselves."*

Maximizing our happiness is so basic that Pascal even asserts that the most miserable person, who commits suicide, is seeking maximum happiness. Such an act is meant to end a person's misery through death, a state assumed to be better for them (ending their unhappiness). Thus death is meant to eliminate a state of miserable unhappiness (thus a happier state—inasmuch as no happiness is to be prefered over unhappiness).

So, I agree with Pascal that we are always pursuing, as much as possible, to maintain and improve our happiness. My additional assertion is that when we strive for too much meaning in our work, we can short circuit our happiness. And I've identified that artists are particularly susceptible to pressing into their work in search of more and more meaning.

Like I said, I'm going to assume that your own experience supports Pascal's observation, that you want to be as happy as you can. I am also going to assume that your own experience as an artist enables you to affirm the premise that artists, more than most, seek meaning and identity from their work.

So what I want to focus on is that middle premise—that seeking too much meaning in work can impede our pursuit of happiness. How exactly does seeking to attach meaning to work make us less happy? And if striving to find too much meaning in work erodes happiness—what's the alternative?

How Seeking Meaningful Work Can Collide with Our Pursuit of Happiness

How does our pursuit of happiness get derailed through striving for too much meaning in work?

In 1969 popular jazz singer Peggy Lee sent the song "Is That All There Is?" to number eleven on the Top 40 hit list. The song is a sober reflection on life, and on those moments when we come to realize how easily we can lose everything we own in a fire, or when we realize that the best moments of life never quite rise to our expectations, or when people we love disappoint us. She hauntingly sang the refrain,

> *"Is that all there is?*
> *If that's all there is my friends*
> *Then let's keep dancing*
> *Let's break out the booze and have a ball*
> *If that's all there is."*

This is a universally nagging question, isn't it? And we really don't like the implications of the question. I am a Christian. I don't believe that this life is all that there is. So for myself I don't hesitate to respond to that question with the answer, "No, this life is not all there is." But even if, like me, you happen to have faith and hope for eternal life, that still leaves us with many years under the sun to figure out our particular purpose in this life. We all want our lives to matter. We all want to make an impact. We all want to contribute to something meaningful, something good, something beautiful. And we want those things to last. Even though we know that our contribution may be small, and barely remembered, if at all, in coming generations.

We still can't escape that refrain, and wonder about our purpose, and whether we're making that positive contribution we yearn for, or how long our contribution might last.

And so the pursuit to answer Peggy Lee's refrain can become vexing. It can produce angst.

Peggy Lee's rendition of "Is that All There Is?" is not quite as morose as some of today's modern-day, nihilistic, punk rock expressions of futility, but it is still pretty bleak. And this is the problem when we connect our pursuit of happiness with the need to find meaning. It can't be answered—at least not with respect to the particular events and situations of our lives. And so the pursuit to answer Peggy Lee's refrain can become vexing. It can produce *angst*.

This angst ridden question of "Is That All There Is?" is so uncomfortable, we spend a great deal of effort avoiding the question altogether! And there are two main ways we do that. First, by outright denial by distraction. We keep busy. We make plans. We fill most of our quiet moments with music, podcasts, Facebook feeds, television, and movies. We try not to think too much about the distant future, and our inevitable final curtain.

But as we get older, we have to start thinking about things like saving for retirement. Retirement planning necessarily involves counting up the decades that we plan to work, and trying to calculate how much we need to invest for the remaining days, those glory years. The older we get, the more we have to think about this. But, for all that financial planning, nobody sets goals for the years *after retirement*. Because there aren't any. We try to put that part out of our minds.

The other way that we distract ourselves from Peggy Lee's nagging question is to focus on justifying the time that we do have. We aim to make the most of these years, and to contribute to something worthwhile. And it's in this effort that we connect our happiness in work with a drive for meaning, and for purpose in our work. If we feel like we've done something, built something, created something, contributed to something bigger than ourselves, then we can console ourselves that at least we've made our lives meaningful. And, indeed, we do make good and beneficial contributions.

But neither distractions nor justifications will push that big question off forever. And sometimes the more this reality weighs on us, the more we lean into those distractions or justifications. And the harder we try, inadequately, to answer this question, the more vexing it can become. Those who are most constantly aware of this inescapable reality, who just can't shake it (particularly as they get older), are the most disturbed by it. And artists, when they wrestle with this reality, due to the very nature of what they do, express these tensions externally, visibly, or audibly—in ways that we can all participate and share in. An accountant can struggle with existential angst, but the tax return he produces will not reflect it. However, this human angst is often revealed in art.

Human Angst Revealed in Art History

If you study art history, you'll find that art, down through the ages, has always reflected thought. Art, in a sense, is visual philosophy. One difference, however, between art and formal philosophy is that the artist is typically working in a creatively *instinctive* way, whereas philosophers engage *cognitively*, with words and ideas, as they attempt to evaluate thoughts with logical precision. Unless you read the works of philosophers, you would never be impacted by their ideas. Artists, on the other hand, give creative expression to these ideas. They make external visual or auditory expressions that we encounter just by occupying the same space without ever having to read a word.

Some fine artists, in particular, engage in the visual expression of ideas and the pursuit of meaning almost as rigorously as philosophers. Fine artists are quite self-conscious about this aspect of their work. Take the work of James Grashow.

An Example from *The Cardboard Bernini*

A great example of this kind of self-conscious, striving angst can be seen in the story of artist James Grashow. The documentary, *The Cardboard Bernini*, tells the story of how he spent four years reproducing, in cardboard, the intricate and expansive fountain designed by baroque artist Gian Bernini. His intention, all along, was to allow his cardboard sculpture to disintegrate with the elements. He intended for it to be displayed, albeit temporarily, *outdoors*. This act of investing all that time in order to let the results fall apart in just a few days was, in part, his desire to express the futility of all work. This short-lived project is a poignant and deliberate illustration of both intense striving for meaning, while acknowledging that nothing lasts forever. The sculpture has long been consigned to the trash heap—but the documentary lasts. (I wonder if he would have been so willing to do this project if it were not being recorded and preserved as a documentary?) But someday that video will be forgotten, too. For that matter, even Bernini's marble sculpture, while having a much longer lifespan than the cardboard version, will eventually crumble.

You're Bringing Me Down, Man!

"Hey, I thought this chapter was supposed to motivate me!" Sorry. I do want to motivate you, and we will come back to the pursuit of happiness and finding joy and satisfaction in your work. But to do that we have to bring this argument full circle. And to do that, I have to drive home the point that there really is a futility in striving for meaning in the details of our lives, and in the work of our hands. Stick with me. We're going to stare this vexing question of meaning square in the face a little longer, until it conquers us. The connection between meaning and work is difficult and painful to break. And until we can dissociate our pursuit of happiness from striving for elusive meaning in our work, we'll never make any more than temporary and superficial progress. So let's let Peggy's refrain echo a couple more times.

Meaning Modified by the Span of Our Lives

Gian Lorenzo Bernini lived from 1598 to 1680. That's a good long life and he's left us many works of art to remember him by. But let's be honest, as an artist you might know the name Bernini, and maybe you could even recognize his works. But most people have no idea who he was. Maybe if you live in Rome and happen to regularly pass by the Piazza di Trevi, you might know the fountain, and maybe you know it was designed by Bernini, but most people have no clue. Gian is long gone.

Jimmy Grashow was born in 1942. He's getting up there in age. I hope he has many more years yet in front of him, and I hope he uses them to create beautiful works of art. But I suspect that in coming generations his mark on art history will be less than Bernini's. Sorry, Jimmy.

Chapter 5: MOTIVATION

Like it or not, in the scheme of things we don't live very long. And it doesn't take long for our memories to be forgotten. Test this. Do you know the name of your great-grandmother and great-grandfather? I hope so. But what about their parents, your great-great-grandparents? How many "greats" would we have to add before you have absolutely no idea? Not many, I suspect. We will be remembered by our children, and hopefully by some of their children, but we all fall off the generational radar pretty quickly in the grand scheme of things, and even the grandkids' memories of us will begin to get fuzzy before we're gone too long. Measured in terms of our memorials, our lives won't amount to much. But don't feel bad, even the most famous are eventually forgotten. It won't take long before iPhone loving teenagers will respond, "Steve Jobs who?"

Meaning Modified by the Extent of Our Impact

Not only are our lives quite short-lived when measured by generations and history, but our reach and impact are also limited. I've lived in Connecticut, Rhode Island, Maryland, and now in North Carolina. I've visited England, the Netherlands, Mexico, the Caribbean, North Africa, and Bahrain. But if you quantified my actual footprint, how much area of each of the specific places I've been, and specific streets I've walked, I've only covered a fraction of a fraction of all the places I could see on Earth. And if I gave completely into wanderlust, and spent all my days traveling to new places, I would not come close to seeing it all.

And since we're getting real, we need to remember that even this vast Earth is but a small planet orbiting a relatively small sun, which is only one of about *a billion* stars in our galaxy. That's right, our galaxy has 1,000,000,000 other stars besides our sun! To even begin to get a sense of scale for how massively large our galaxy is with its one billion stars, consider that it would take 100,000 years traveling *at the speed of light* to cross the expanse of our Milky Way galaxy. I am very small.

But here's the truly mind-blowing reality. Go outside some night and, taking a drinking straw, hold it at arm's length and look through it at any point in the night sky. Did you know that in that pea-sized sector of the night sky, if you could zoom way in on just that small spot with a powerful telescope, you would see 11,000 more points of light? That's 11,000 in that small spot! But here's the thing, those 11,000 lights are not other stars inside our galaxy. They're galaxies of their own! Each one containing a billion stars. Eleven thousand galaxies each with a billion suns, in that one tiny spot in the night sky! I know, it's mind-boggling. We are very small.

Where Motivation Can Be Found

If we try to measure our meaning by the memories we'll leave behind, or by the impact we'll make on the world—the expanse of history, and the expanse of the universe will shrink our meaning down to particles so small as to be essentially meaningless. If we get even a glimpse of proper perspective, our desire to strive for meaning will always lead to vexation, we will be angst-ridden indeed.

Is Artistic Angst a Blessing or a Curse?

James Grashow, in *The Cardboard Bernini*, expressed this kind of angst in the very design of his project, but he also expresses it verbally in the film.

> *"In the beginning of my career, if my work was cherished, what I feel about eternity, or what I feel about the future, would be different. I'm still looking for the truth of myself . . . but I still find that truth very, very elusive."*

The meaning of his work, measured against eternity, was, and is, and always will be, very elusive. But even though it's elusive, James seems to need that angst. It's a part of his artistic process, even though it never finds an endpoint or an answer. When his cardboard project was finished and delivered, reflecting on its completion he muses,

> *"I'm starting to percolate again, which I didn't think was going to happen . . . I was thinking about where I was going to go, and what I was going to do, and just the emptiness of life. Which is ridiculous for me . . . I have a great home, wife, and grandkids—how is it possible that I was still miserable? I was just ridiculous. I was sitting in this auditorium alone, with my head down, asking myself these questions: What am I going to do? Who am I? What does it all mean anyway? I mean what does it all mean, all of the amount of work that you do if you come up empty in the end anyway? So what does it mean?*
>
> *And then I looked down onto the floor, in this gigantic auditorium—I had chosen a seat and right at my foot was a pencil, this little pencil. I think, I don't know, God, my mother, somebody, some ancestor put that pencil there. I don't know if it was there when I sat down. But it seemed to be the answer. That the only thing that I could do is what I had done, which is to continue to work. That's what I was supposed to do. That was my mission—to make art, to make stuff, and that I should just keep doing it."*

For James his angst is the fuel that keeps his work going. It's both his fuel and his purpose. His purpose is to create art. The art expresses futility. The futility answers with a call to return to the work. His art is a cycle of angst.

Jimmy mentions how his angst and his circumstances don't really match up. He has a beautiful home, wife, and grandkids. His wife makes a key observation about this incongruity. Because they were so happily married she quipped during an interview, with a knowing smile, the irony that, "Jimmy says I robbed him of his misery."

James Grashow knows, at least for his own experience, that he needs his angst. It drives his creative process. And so in one sense, if we value the product of artistic endeavor, which flows out from this energy of artistic angst, we would not want to take that away—we don't want to rob artists of their misery. But if we are meant to pursue happiness, we have a real dilemma, don't we?

Replacing the Pursuit of Meaning with the Pursuit of Goodness

If the pressures of eternity, purpose, and meaning find their outlet and expression in our work, as is common for creatives, we are going to be vexed and unhappy—even if we come to terms with it. Yet it seems, from the common experience, so well documented in *The Cardboard Bernini*, that artists need that energy, that fuel, that pressure that comes from angst because it seems to drive the creative process. But does our fuel have to consist of angst-ridden pursuits of meaning?

No it does not. And this is the key. If you want to be motivated, fueled, and energized in your work—if you want to be moving toward happiness—you're going to have to swap out the drive for meaning with the drive for something else. And that something else is *goodness*.

Meaning and purpose, when measured by our legacy, or our impact, is so small and elusive that it always generates unanswerable questions and unresolvable angst. That's because meaning and purpose, evaluated this way, are measured by their size. How long will people remember us? How deep will our impact be? How much change will we inspire? Meaning measured in these ways is quantitative (how long, how deep). And, if we're honest and use proper scales, these quantities are far too infinitesimal to ever be satisfying for our souls. *Goodness*, however is not a quantity, it's a *quality*. And being a quality, it's relative size does not matter. If you try to stretch your arms out to the nearest star—you will never reach it, you'll always fall short. But if you do something good, even a small thing, it is still good—its size is not a qualifier for its being good.

Do you see what a big difference this is? If we measure by meaning, and judge it quantitatively, then falling short means failure. If your goal is to be remembered for one hundred years, and you are forgotten within a decade, you fail to reach your goal. But if your measure is qualitative, if you seek to do good, then regardless of how small an act of goodness may be, it's still good—it does not fail to be good. It retains its quality. Being motivated to simply do good will result in less angst than being motivated by striving for meaning.

In making the swap from meaning to goodness, or in my motivating you to do so, please don't think that my intention to detach your motivations from seeking meaning to seeking goodness is somehow a denial that meaning in work exists at all. I do believe that work is meaningful, and does make an important contribution. The problem isn't in the reality, it's in our capacity to connect daily work to those questions. Those big questions are real and important. And finding answers is a worthy pursuit. I am saying that the attempt to locate that meaning, in and through our work, is impossible due to scale, and as a result, our futile efforts to find that meaning leave us empty. Unless we become aware of this tendency, to seek too much meaning in work, we will find ourselves falling prey to it. In order to escape it, we need to intentionally, consciously, and constantly redirect our motives from seeking meaning in work, to enjoying the simple satisfaction that we have done good work, and then to enjoy the rewards that come from work well done.

The Joys of Attaining Redirected Ends

When you change your aim, looking not for grandiose answers to life the universe and everything, but rather content yourself with doing good work, you can experience rewards every day. Instead of leaving the studio vexed and disturbed, you can leave reflecting on having done the job, completed (hopefully) your tasks, delivered good work (or contributed to it), and having served your clients well. That is a truly satisfying inner reward that can be delivered every day. And that, coupled with the financial expressions of good, valuable work, amplify these rewards and begin to deliver on our pursuit of happiness.

Diagnosing Angst in Your Practice

Now most creative professionals don't show up for work every day tied up in Gordian Knots of artistic angst like James Grashow seems to need. But all artists and designers can relate to these tensions at some level. Angst is always buzzing to some degree. And it does affect how we engage our work.

In the next chapter, as we return to the topic of Management working backward through the first four Ms, I'm going to introduce you to the DiSC profile. It's a useful tool that can make you more self aware about your work tendencies and temperament, and how some tasks will stand in tension with your suitability. A DiSC report can't fix those tensions. But it can help us anticipate when, and under what circumstances, we'll need to adapt. Unfortunately, the DiSC profile does not measure creative angst. Since we don't have a DiSC report for angst, the best we can do is recognize that we all face this artistic occupational hazard to some extent. Knowing it's there, and recognizing the dangers it creates, our self-awareness can help us to readjust our ambitions from striving for meaning to simply doing good and temper our angst.

Added Benefits of an Adjusted Motivation

There are added benefits to swapping out the engine of angst for the propeller of goodness. When you become more motivated by the desire to simply do good, to work hard, and to produce value, your ability to satisfy that goal can be met in any kind of work! The nature of the task does not limit the pursuit of goodness. If motivation is tied to meaning, then you may despise putting down the paintbrush in order to engage in prospecting. You will dread closing Photoshop in order to plan your upcoming production calendar.

When you have to function in the various noncreative aspects of your business, artistic angst will always hinder you. This may help explain why most artists and designers react so negatively to the noncreative aspects of their business. Where is the pursuit and expression of meaning in a financial report? Sometimes the creative drive for meaning gets so thoroughly in the way, artists neglect business fundamentals entirely. That never ends well.

But if you can detach from a demand to discover meaning and find satisfaction in the goodness of what you are doing day by day, you may discover that you can capture some of that same satisfaction you get from your artistic work in the noncreative aspects of running your business. If you can release the demand that your work result in elusive "meaning," then you can begin to find some pleasure in all your work, whether it's a layout, a logo, or evaluating line items on your budget.

I wrote this book because I want to help owners of creative service practices overcome the creative tensions they wrestle with in their work. The business aspects of creativity—cash flow, client conflicts, marketing fatigue, employee problems—can make joy in their work even more scarce. The basic goal of this book is to train creatives in the fundamentals of running a business. But I hope it can accomplish something deeper—to restore the elusive enjoyment of work—to more fully reward your toil.

Gearing Up for the Path Ahead

Congratulations, you've made it to the summit. From this altitude, you can see your practice from a whole new perspective. And now it's time to blaze your trail back to stable ground. As I emphasized in chapter three on marketing, narrow positioning is critical for effective marketing. But it's also a lynchpin for the whole book. As we move now into the more pragmatic, practical, and tactical part of the book and talk about implementation, I want you to think about how following my advice to position narrowly might minimize the amount of work involved in implementing the systemic changes we'll discuss. You see, narrow positioning is not just key for effective marketing, it also streamlines and focuses your entire practice. For each of the topics, systems, practices we'll discuss next, a creative firm that has narrowed their focus to one main industry and one main product will find implementation easier at every point. On the other hand implementing from a generalist position will require more breadth and coverage to every system and practice—making tactical improvements harder to make.

Let me give you one example of how the five principles connect and work better when operating in a narrowly positioned practice. Let's connect some dots between Money and Minutes.

Managing your money and your time are, indeed, necessary and important habits for running a successful business. But managing money for a generalist company, like a local grocery store, for example, takes more effort than for, in contrast, a specialty shop. Whereas a grocery store has thousands of SKUs to maintain, and constantly cycling inventory, a specialty store can keep a smaller catalog of products, and reduce its total inventory.

Generalist creatives, like general stores, offer a wide range of services: print, advertising, collateral, copywriting, signs, web, video, and so on. And for every kind of service there is a unique set of requirements, processes, and cost parameters. Maintaining a long list of services to a broad range of clients compounds the effort needed to managing your money and your minutes.

But if you focus on one kind of service, for one primary client type, all of your business practices will start to settle into fewer and more predictable processes. When you repeatedly perform similar services for similar clients, your expertise and in-depth understanding of all that goes into fulfilling these services makes the behind-the-scenes effort to manage them easier and easier. Your billing practices will be simplified. Your project schedules will be constant from project to project. And your client's needs will be increasingly familiar to you.

The generalist position is an uphill battle for marketing, and can be an impossible mess to manage. The narrow specialist positioning is a sustainable upward spiral of control, profitability, and effectiveness. Running a successful creative service will always be challenging, but when you commit to focus rather than frenzy, the necessary toil will reduce to reasonable levels, and the rewards will flow more freely.

So as you begin blazing your trail back down this mountain, if you start to feel overwhelmed, keep reflecting on how applying these strategies, practices, and systems might not be as daunting if you opt-in to the key principle of narrow positioning.

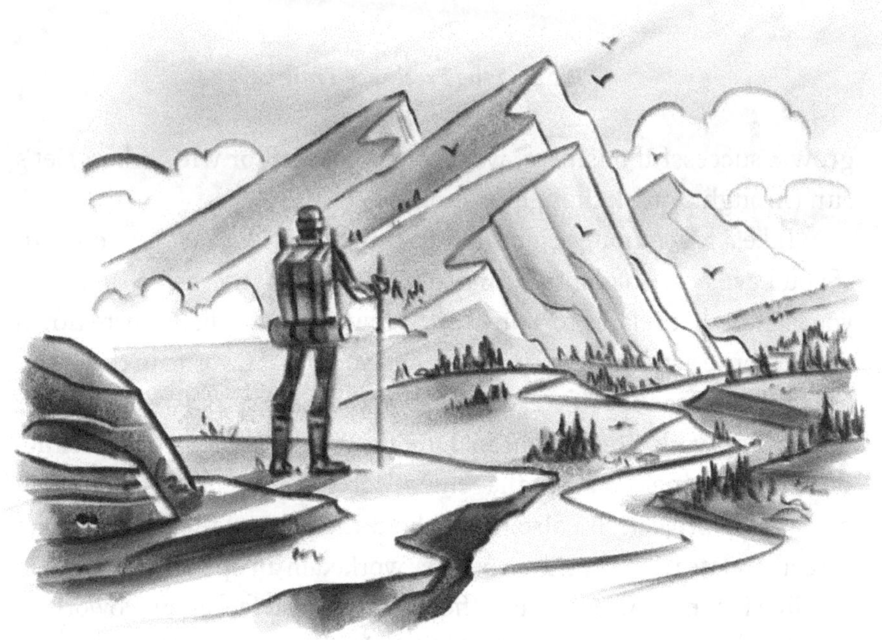

Chapter 6: MANAGEMENT in Practice

As I discussed in the first Management chapter, it is important, from day one, to think through whether you will grow your practice into a multiperson business, or remain a solo practitioner. How you manage yourself, your marketing, your minutes, and your money can take different forms depending on your intentions.

After you give this serious thought, and once you establish at least your desires and intentions for which path you'd like to follow, you may want to pursue an objective assessment about your abilities to function optimally in either a long-term solo practice, or as the leader of a growing company. Understanding your work-style and temperament can identify which roles you are most comfortable filling yourself, and which ones will be particularly challenging. And if you do end up going down the scalable business path, then you'll need to consider which roles to hire for (and when to hire them) based on your assessment. Before we dig into the specific roles that are required to grow a successful business, whether by yourself or with others, let's run through a quick thought exercise.

Take a few minutes right now to think about the last job you had. If you have never had a full-time job, think of an internship or a class you've had that relates to your work. Now make two lists: write down your favorite aspects of work in one, and your least favorite in the other. Make the lists as specific as possible, and consider all aspects of your day-to-day work. They might include practical functions like writing, designing, using project management software, or collaborating with others on a project. But also think about the parts of the job that don't directly relate to work. Have you ever worked in an open floor plan? Do you like having coffee in your office? How do you feel about coworkers and incidental meetings in the kitchen? What about communicating with clients?

After you've taken some time to think about the range of tasks, roles, and environmental preferences, ask yourself whether any of these preferences indicate which path is optimal. This chapter will describe in more detail some of the basic roles and functions needed to run any business, whether solo or scaling. Try to be honest in your self-assessment as you contemplate these roles and picture yourself in them, and how you will fare in them over time.

How to Wear All the Hats Without Hiring

This book is intended as a guide for the creative freelancer. But I also want to lay out the path of turning a freelance practice into a growing firm—since that happens to many successful freelancers. Since this chapter is going to focus on different roles, it's important to note that in a multiperson practice, these roles are filled by *different people*. And not different people in general, but each role is best suited to those with skills, temperaments, and strengths that match them. In fact, some of the traits that make one individual well-suited to one role may make them quite unsuitable for another. And this is one of the biggest challenges in running a solo practice. You alone have to fulfill every role. Yet, as one person, with a definite set of strengths and weaknesses, it's virtually assured that you will not be well-suited for every role you have to fulfill. That means there are certain tasks and functions *that you are not well-suited for!* But you have to do them anyway. Understanding what these roles are and how you can fill them—even when they don't play to your strengths—is part of *managing your practice well.*

So let's walk through each of these roles, describe their functions, and consider how you can optimally perform each one without neglecting their core functions. The main roles we will explore are: Production, Administration, Client Services, and New Business.

> *It's virtually assured that you will not be well-suited for every role you have to fulfill.*

The Production Role

The production of art, design, and other forms of creative content is why you got into this career in the first place. It's what you know best. It's probably the thing that you wish you could be doing more of, and is the thing successful freelancers want to recapture when they contemplate hiring help. The first thing to remember about this essential part of your business is that, as a freelancer, your production capacity will be limited to not much more than 60% of your overall available time (we'll review this percentage in chapter 8). And keep in mind that about 20% of that production time will likely be taken up with client communications and meetings. That will only leave you with about half of your week for creative productivity. This is a real limitation. If you try to steal more time from the other roles, in order to focus more on creating, you will impair the long-term health of your company.

So as a manager of yourself, you're going to need to begin by adjusting your expectations of how much of your overall time can be devoted to creative work. You have to accept that being a freelancer means that you are both a creative producer and a businessperson. And you have to give yourself to both aspects if you're going to be successful. If you really can't live with this adjusted expectation, you may want to seriously consider working for a firm. Staff creatives can focus 80% or more of their time on the creative work itself.

In addition to adapting your expectations, you will also need to manage your calendar so that you can make the most of the twenty to twenty-five hours per week you can devote to production. Production does require significant concentration. You can't be on call, and checking your email, and getting texts while engaged in the deep work of production. You can't afford distractions when you can only devote about half your time to creative work to begin with.

This is why managing your calendar (more on this also in chapter 8) is such an important managerial skill and discipline. You need to plan your days and set aside blocks of hours in order to focus on creativity. You'll need to plan times when you commit to turning off email and silencing your phone in order to dive into the creative process. Establishing some regular patterns for these blocks of time will not only help you maximize productivity, but a regular routine will serve your clients as well. If you can communicate these times, so that they know that you will not be available, they can adjust their own expectations for communication. You might even consider using voice mail messages and auto responders during your work periods, to inform your clients that "you're in the studio right now" and note when you plan on "returning to the office" to respond to messages. Even if "your studio" is your computer, which is the same physical space as "your office," you should try to conceive of your production time as if you're a painter who has to leave the office and go into the studio to work. When you're at work, you should be unreachable. Yet professionalism demands that you clearly communicate your availability to clients.

While you will need to learn some new skills and disciplines for managing your production time, the essence of your work is what you're most suited for, so apart from securing the time to do it, the work itself will come naturally.

But that is probably not the case with some of the other important functions that you need to engage in, particularly the administrative functions of running a business.

Administrative Roles

The administrative aspects of running your practice are among the least preferred, and probably least suited to your skills and temperament. Many of the practical aspects of these principles are designed to help you implement processes, systems, and procedures in these areas. But the administrative functions are pretty broad, so we need to break them down.

1. Bookkeeping and Finances. Managing the finances is the most easily and commonly outsourced aspect of a freelance business, and that's fine—so long as you fully understand your financial instruments and your bookkeeper provides monthly balance sheets, P&Ls, and that you keep up with your cash flow spreadsheet (more on these in chapter 9). On the other hand, if you set up your systems well and keep up with them weekly, this is one of the easiest things for you to do yourself. And learning how to do this yourself will save you some money with the added benefit of keeping your hand on the pulse of your financial health on a regular basis.

But once you've mastered these instruments, and understand how they work—and once you have sufficient profits, bookkeeping tasks are one area you may be able to outsource, without hiring an employee, in order to regain a bit more time for art and design.

2. Evaluating Financial and Time Data. In the section on "Minutes," we hammered home how important it is to keep comprehensive and accurate time records of *all your work* (including the time you spend evaluating time metrics!). Assuming you've entered your time each day, and that you've developed meaningful time categories, pulling reports for analysis is a simple process.

The unpleasant but necessary work is entering all your time daily. It doesn't take much time, just daily discipline and diligence. Reticence to daily, accurate timekeeping probably has more to do with motivational creative tensions described in chapter 5 than anything functional. You have to do this.

In a multiperson firm, timesheet compliance is given to someone who is responsible for the overall profitability of a project. A traffic manager or production manager is often a good fit for this task. Because daily time tracking and entry are so important, this task is one that requires some degree of unpleasant prodding and account-ability systems (rewards and consequences). But if you work alone, how do you prod yourself? You may need to get creative on this front. It's too tempting, at the end of a long day, to go easy on yourself and not enter your time. Perhaps you can ask a friend to hold you accountable. Give them twenty dollars (or whatever amount would hurt if you lost it) and ask them to simply check your timekeeping system each evening to make sure you logged a complete day's worth of time. If you didn't log your time, your friend keeps the twenty dollars, and you give them another twenty dollars to continue keeping you accountable. If that doesn't work, give them a Benjamin. I assure you there is a cost that will get you to comply. You might need to figure out what that cost is—and I'm sure your friend will be happy to explore that with you!

3. Estimating and Scheduling (Coordination). In larger advertising agencies the function of estimating and scheduling falls under the role of the production or traffic manager. This important role is one that the freelance artist or designer may find difficult to perform. It requires a data-driven mind that balances lots of detail (characteristics which most creative types lack). The output of the estimating and scheduling function (quotes for new projects, timelines, and schedules) needs to be grounded in cold hard facts and solid time data. The output should not be fudged, or involve subjective guessing, or wishful thinking.

There is an additional reason why solo practitioners find this function difficult (even if they happen to have a high threshold for data and details). Since the output of this data analysis determines budgets and schedules, an overeagerness to close new business, or to please existing clients, or even just the allure of a creative opportunity can easily distort your cost estimations. These kinds of pressures can cause us to paint optimistic scenarios in order to justify lower fees, or to agree to aggressive schedules. As a result, it is best to separate the administrative function of estimating and scheduling from the function of client service and new business. In firms with multiple employees, the estimating and scheduling role should be delegated to someone with the right mind-set, temperament, and skills who is not being pressured by client demands or desperate sales conditions.

This kind of role separation creates a serious dilemma for the freelancer since you can't divvy up these roles to different people. However, there are some things you can do to help avoid the tensions and downward pressures of having to engage in new business, provide client service, and also perform these analytical functions yourself.

First of all, make sure that you have the data you need to analyze and evaluate in order to come up with sound quotes and schedules in the first place. Keep your timesheets! (I know, I'm a broken record, but you have to have this valuable data.)

Secondly, while you can't separate the roles by giving them to different people, you can *create distance* between the times at which you perform these functions. *Never give quotes or schedules during meetings or in conversations with clients!* Always defer to your process when you are asked for a quote or an estimate. Get used to saying, something like,

> *"I never give quotes, or agree to schedules, until I've sat down with my resourcing data so I can balance all my clients' needs, and all my*

> *projects, responsibly. I typically do my scheduling and quoting on Friday mornings, so I'll have an answer for you by Friday afternoon."*

If a client really presses, promise to move your resourcing schedule up in order to get them a quote faster—but never give them the quote on the spot. Instead of separating these functions with different people, create separation between the times when you perform the tasks of client service, new business, and when you determine your quotes and schedules.

Additionally, when you start estimating, take a moment to mentally change hats. Check your client service and sales hats at the door, and put on a detective's hat, in order to solve your calendar puzzle, and search past projects that will give you a realistic gauge for estimating new work. When we revisit Minutes, I'll have some recommendations for software that can help with these tasks. But one tip to consider for now, after you've come up with your best data-driven estimate—double it, or if you have the guts, triple it. You will always need some metric to compensate for your innate bias toward unrealistic optimism of your capabilities and your inability to predict when and how projects will encounter unanticipated snags.

When you start estimating, take a moment to mentally change hats.

Only after doing your best to fit all your deadlines and dependencies into your schedule, should you deliver quotes and schedules to clients. And when you do, it would be best to provide them in a formal document that conveys the fact that the quote is based on data (though you should not provide all the details). It will be harder for your clients to push back when they know that your quotes are based on hard data. Likewise, it will be easier for you to stick to your guns when you know that your numbers aren't hanging in the air, but that you really need that much time to deliver quality in a sustainable and profitable way, for the benefit of all your clients.

Client Service Roles

Every freelancer must interact with their clients. How suited you may be for this function is a toss up. Whereas all artists are going to be well-suited to the production role by definition, and it's usually the case that most artists struggle with their administrative functions, how you relate to your clients can go either way. There is nothing inherent to artistic talent that makes one an introvert or an extrovert, conversational or withdrawn. Some artists and designers thrive in client meetings and phone calls. Others would prefer to avoid them. But the client service function is baked into this business. For those who are not inclined to client relationships, you have to overcome those barriers. And for those who do crave these interactions, you may need to remember that you're a professional delivering a product to a client, and resist the urge to make every client your best friend (best friends make terrible clients).

I've mentioned the DiSC profile a couple times already. Your DiSC profile can indicate which roles and functions will come naturally to you and which ones you may be tempted to ignore. For certain roles, like production, many different profiles fit just fine. But for others, like the client service role, the presence or absence of certain patterns are highly suggestive of how a person will perform in client-facing circumstances. For example, if you have a high "I" ("I" stands for Influence, or how you relate to other people) you will find customer service one of the highlights of your job. But if you have a low "I," you may dread it every time you have to engage personally with a client (especially if you have a conflict with them). Another example: if you have a high "S" score (Stability, a preference for structure and predictable processes), you might have no problem with systemic solutions like time-tracking and keeping your books. The idea of predictable routines and schedules appeals to a high "S." But a low "S" may dread the idea of scheduling and measuring minutes. A high "C" (Conscientiousness, attention to detail, data driven) won't be at all intimidated by time data analysis or working out project schedules and quotes. But a low "C" might prefer root canal to opening up QuickBooks.

DiSC profiles will help predict where you will function naturally, and where things will be harder. But they are rarely indicators of whether you can perform in certain roles at all. We all have to operate outside of our comfort zones from time to time. And while we might not like it, and while being outside our comfort zones might drain our energy, we can still do it. The DiSC report increases your self-awareness. Knowing what your strengths and weaknesses are, what your tendencies and temperament are toward work—what challenges you may face—can help you overcome obstacles and function in roles that will take more energy.

Aside from personal temperament, there are other challenges with client service in its relationship to other roles. Just as certain administrative functions, like estimating and scheduling, are best separated from new business and client service, there is also a built-in tension between client service and other roles, particularly production and new business. These tensions have to do with *availability*. When it comes to customer satisfaction from your service (not just your product), availability and timely communications are key. In a multiperson firm, client service is a dedicated function, and people in that role spend most of their days interacting with clients, emailing them, and coordinating with them. They can, and should, be available to respond quickly to client inquiries.

But this kind of high-touch, quick-response communication can have a serious drain on the efficiency of the production role—constant emails are a huge concentration killer. Even as I'm writing this, I've got my door locked, my email tab closed, and phone on airplane mode to avoid unnecessary interruptions and distractions. But this kind of necessary isolation, to think and to create, is in tension with your client's need to get in touch with you in a timely manner.

How can you overcome these tensions? As described above you can develop consistent studio habits by setting aside certain days of the week, or certain blocks of hours for production. While you'll never be able to craft a perfectly consistent weekly schedule that never bends, if you don't set some boundaries, you may compromise the focused time you need for deep work. But if you maintain consistent studio hours, your clients will come to know that while you may be unavailable at certain times of the week, they can count on hearing back from you on a regular and predictable basis.

Client service is one area where, if you are profitable enough, you could make a hire in order to gain more time for creative production. But since the ratio of client service to production time is something like 1:4 you'd have to be very profitable to hire someone to cover the 20 percent of client service work that your base level productivity will demand. One common solution (or supposed solution) to hiring an account manager, even though there is not enough work to justify a full-time role, is to hire someone to handle both customer service as well as some new business work. This seems like a perfect solution, but it rarely works out, and that's because there are inevitable tensions between the customer service role and the new business role.

> *There are inevitable tensions between the customer service role and the new business role.*

Marketing and New Business Roles

Perhaps even more than the reluctance creative freelancers feel toward administrative duties, marketing and new business are even less attractive, especially when these efforts bear little fruit due to marketing from a generalist position. But even if you fix that and cultivate a narrow position from which you can find, approach, and persuade prospects to become new clients, it will still involve ongoing effort to maintain your marketing. Rarely is marketing work attractive to an artist—we'd rather stay in the studio creating. We are loathe to close our sketchbooks and to lean into the mundane task of identifying prospects and adding them into a customer relationship management system. Marketing involves outbound email campaigns, qualifying prospects, and evaluating opportunities. Some of this work is simply dull. Reviewing profiles and adding them to a database can be monotonous. In the early stages of cultivating your positioning, you'll need to do a significant amount of this kind of toil. But as time goes on and your presence and reputation within your market grows, you may get to the point where you have more inbound leads than you can respond to. This is the ultimate goal of marketing and the evidence of its success. Whatever stage your marketing is at, you'll need to spend time on it—and you'll probably find every reason not to settle down to do it. It's going to take some basic self-discipline and resolve to stick to your marketing plan.

Without doing the hard work of positioning first, even the most well-intentioned and disciplined efforts fail from lack of results and discouragement. A solid positioning will improve your results—but not without the necessary elbow grease. In the words of Roger Miller, when it comes to your marketing plan, you need to "knuckle down, buckle down, do it, do it, do it."

Some artists just don't want to do it. And, so the idea of hiring an account manager, *who also agrees to take on marketing*, seems like the perfect solution to kill two birds with one stone. But it rarely works out. First, because of the availability issue. A client-service person, who redirects their efforts to find new leads, will not be as accessible to clients as a dedicated account manager would be. Additionally, the DiSC profiles that tend to indicate sales competency are distinct from that of a good customer service representative.

On top of all that, the motivations of new business professionals are different from customer service professionals. A true salesperson wants to make money (that's why they are open to commission arrangements). But if they are bogged down answering clients' emails and phone calls, they can't be landing juicy new accounts. On the other hand, if someone is cut out for the account management role, and is highly motivated to please clients, they will likely dread the hard work of having to find clients (probably as much as you do). They might agree to do it, but they are rarely successful at it. They are always too busy with the needs of their clients to set aside time for marketing. For this reason, they will be less inclined to make commissions a significant aspect of their compensation. They will want a solid base salary and would view the commission structure as a nice bonus, if they happen to get anything, but not be motivated by need (and opportunity) to get out there and find good clients—the way a true new business development person would be.

For these reasons, in a creative firm, it's best not to combine these roles. But when it comes to fulfilling them yourself, as a solo creative freelancer, you'll need to use careful scheduling to integrate the production and customer service functions. And you'll need good old-fashioned resolve and discipline to put in your hours working your marketing program, digging through LinkedIn, and sending emails.

Tips for Disciplined Hat Swapping

As a freelance creative entrepreneur, you're going to have to fulfill all the distinct functions and roles—including those that are not best suited to the artistic temperament, and even those that ideally ought to be fulfilled by someone else. Keeping your practice healthy and in balance will require significant discipline. There are plenty of resources out there along the lines of Stephen Covey's *The 7 Habits of Successful People*. But I'll summarize some of the solutions offered so far, and add a few more suggestions for the creative's need to be disciplined in business.

1. Define Your Structures and Processes: When it comes to tasks like bookkeeping, time management, resource analysis, marketing plans, and such, having regular times set aside for these tasks can help you maintain proper attention to these functions. If you've spent weeks neglecting your bank statements, not paying your bills, and ignoring your cash flow, then getting back into it will require facing a real mountain of work. The prospect of digging in can be so daunting that you may decide to ignore it for yet another week—making the mountain even bigger. And so you need to set *and keep* regular rhythms and processes for doing these tasks so that the steps involved, and the routines you use, become second nature.

It may be worth spending time cleaning up your accounts, tightening up your categories, and establishing a step-by-step process for each of these administrative tasks, so that you can have at it, and get it done as quickly and easily as possible on a weekly basis. When I was managing my first firm, there was no QuickBooks online. I had to manually print and mail invoices every week and process receivables by hand. I would come in early, or stay late, or maybe set aside a Saturday morning when the office was quiet to make the process as enjoyable as possible. Today, as CEO of Cuberis, I still handle all the billing and finances. But with all the online systems available, I can process and update everything in about an hour each Friday morning.

2. Do the Hard Tasks First: If you have a set of tasks to get done each day, and some are more appealing than others, prioritize the least pleasant items first. If you intend to spend an hour and a half implementing your marketing system, do that first before going into the studio or booting up Photoshop. You'll probably find that your creativity is improved, having already done the hard part. On the other hand, creativity is hampered when you know that there is a mountain of administrative work piling up or some less pleasant marketing work ahead of you.

3. Establish an Aesthetically Pleasing Environment: When tackling the less-attractive administrative or marketing tasks, try to make your environment as pleasant as possible. Put on some music, maybe straighten up your desk, crack open a refreshing beverage. Don't make these necessary aspects of your job any harder than they need to be by trying to get them done with distractions and clutter to demotivate you.

4. Consider How All The Toil Really Does Serve The Creative Product: A well-managed practice will result in greater stability and profitability. When you know that you have money in the bank, when you know that your administrative tasks are up-to-date, you will produce better work. When you are not managing yourself well, and you're striving financially, and struggling for new business, and letting the paperwork pile up—you will not produce your best work. It's true that diving into administrative and marketing tasks may feel antithetical to the creative process, but keeping these aspects up-to-date will free you and improve your ability to produce beautiful and effective work. Your ability to focus, with a clear mind that's not stressed by financial worries and slipping deadlines, will serve your creative effectiveness.

Chapter 6: MANAGEMENT
Summary and Assignments

1.   Have you ever flirted with the idea of hiring help? What holds you back from that decision? Under what conditions might you consider hiring an employee? How have the cautions offered in the chapters on management adjusted your decision-making process?

2.   If you ever feel overworked or burned out, how might you be able to determine if the cause is coming from a lack of profitability?

3.   Have you ever said "no" to a client or project that was offered to you? Why or why not? Are there any potential projects coming up that you know that you ought to say "no" to? What fears might cause you to say "yes" when you know you should say "no?" What criteria can you apply to potential new clients or projects that would provide an objective grid for deciding when you ought to say "no" to a piece of new business?

4. Are you able to adapt to the limiting idea that only about half of your overall work time can be used for creative production?

5. Which hats do you find hardest to wear among all the roles in running your practice? Do these struggles map predictably to your DiSC profile? How can understanding your profile help you face those tasks and functions that you are least suitable for?

6. Are you a disciplined person by nature? If not, what kinds of management ideas might you need to employ (like giving money to a friend to help you keep your timesheets up-to-date) in order to hold yourself accountable for the business tasks you need to be performing regularly?

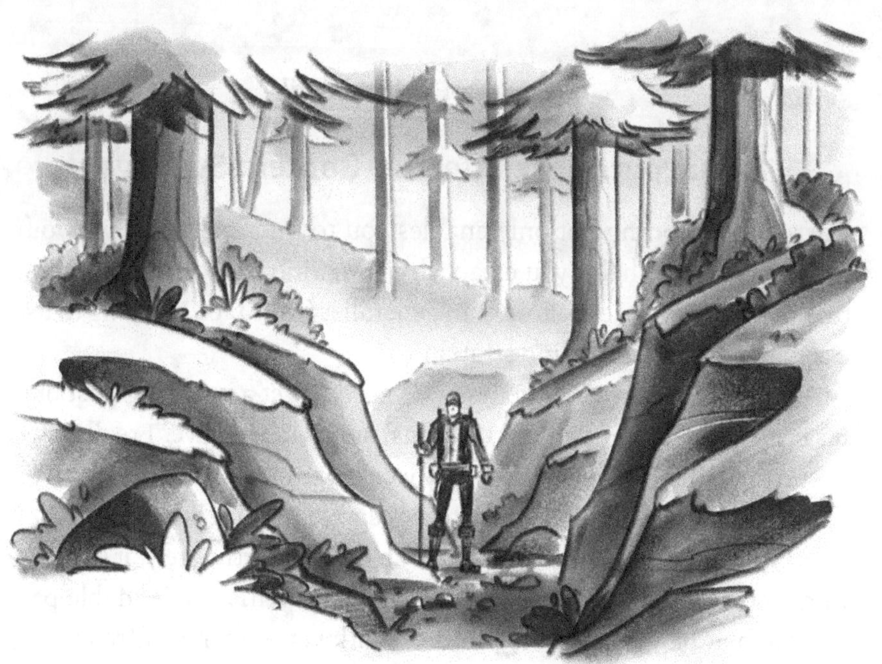

Chapter 7: MARKETING in Practice

I am a big proponent of content marketing. There are countless benefits to creating a steady flow of content on your blog, in a newsletter, or through social media. And while the concept of content marketing is easy to grasp, it can be surprisingly challenging to pull off.

To illustrate this point, try this simple exercise. Take five minutes right now to write the title and opening paragraph of a blog post. It can be about anything at all. And if you've already got the first one in the chamber, try coming up with the titles of a few more.

If you had any trouble with that, consider what it might take to write one blog post a week throughout the life of your business. You may fear running out of ideas in the first year. And even if you are good at coming up with regular ideas to write about, how effective will that content be? Will qualified prospects find and be persuaded by your content?

While the basic concept of content marketing is simple, successful execution is rare. That is, unless you've established your narrow *positioning*.

A Sharper, More Effective Content Strategy

Narrow positioning not only enables you to find and persuade your prospects, it also helps you establish and maintain a content strategy that performs with less effort than generalist firms face in trying to use a content-driven marketing strategy.

Have you ever said to yourself, "I need to get a new blog post out. It's been a month, no wait, two months, or has it been five? I really need to start putting out new posts every week, or at least once a month. I'll put that on my calendar, right after I respond to this client's email . . ."

I've looked at a lot of design firm blogs. Unfortunately, it's rare to find a creative's website that's using its blog well. A dependable pattern to their blogs is that they start off with some degree of frequency, maybe weekly, but then they slow down to monthly, then quarterly, and then stop.

Unfortunately, it's rare to find a creative's website that's using its blog well.

Why is this such a common trend? A friend of mine has a favorite expression that fits a creative freelancer's blogging experience, "The juice just isn't worth the squeeze."

Blogging takes time. And freelancers don't have tons of that to spare. Making the time to squeeze fresh content into a blog comes at a high cost. And when that time investment doesn't seem to be paying off—the juice just isn't worth the squeeze.

This is a sad reality since a blog (or a newsletter, or some other form of regular written content) can be a powerful business development tool for a creative professional. But making it work is not simply a factor of adding more content, rather it means adding the *right kind of content*.

The Wrong Kind of Content

Here are the things that your blog should not be full of: design tips, favorite typefaces, web development tips, new clients won, new hires, your opinion about the latest Netflix original, your pets, employee profiles, or your holiday party photos. Now don't get me wrong, a few of those kinds of posts are fine from time to time—but if these make up the majority of your content, *you're doing it wrong.*

Your blog's content should be one of the most persuasive components of your site. And while you might think your prospects are interested in the latest fonts from the Monotype catalog, or efficient Photoshop hacks, they're not. That kind of content might be of interest to other designers, but not to your prospects. So unless the primary goal for your blog is recruitment, such content should not be the mainstay of your blogging diet.

The Right Kind of Blog Content

So if not posts about fonts and felines, what should you write about? Write things that interest your prospects. What would compel them to hire you? Trying to answer this question exposes the fundamental positioning problem of most freelance blogs—they don't know who their prospective client might be. It exposes their positioning problem.

When your potential client could be a business, or nonprofit, or institution who needs web work, or print work, or identity design, or advertising, or packaging—it's almost impossible to find a focus for a sustainable editorial calendar.

And you have to multiply all the services you offer by the number of industries you might serve and that's how many potential client profiles you have to consider when you're trying to come up with an editorial strategy for your blog. No wonder so many creative freelance blogs fail!

Benefits of a Focused Blog Strategy

But when clients find a creative professional's website and it answers *their particular needs,* the blog can do almost all the selling. And not only that, by virtue of the nature of blog content, there is a high degree of likelihood that such potential clients might very well stumble upon your content through search engine activity, as their focused search parameters match your focused content.

And the more your expertise grows, the easier it is to produce persuasive content. A new upward cycle will reverse the downward spiral of languishing ineffective posts.

That's a whole lot more juice with a lot less squeezing.

Narrow Positioning Exercise

This exercise will help you connect the dots between narrow positioning and effective and sustainable content strategy.

Fill in each of the blanks of this generic positioning statement with a highly focused, limited set of options that you could imagine making a focus for a profitable practice. The wording is generic, but an actual positioning statement must contain these three main parts. If you remember from chapter 3, a narrow positioning statement must answer three main questions: what you do, who you do it for, and how it benefits them. Blanks one and two below are facets of the first question, and blanks three and four answer the second and third main questions respectively.

Try to come up with three different possibilities by filing in the blanks below.

______ is a ______ that provides ______, for companies in the ______ industry, so that our clients gain ______.

The first two blanks simply state your name and your general practice type (design, illustration, copy-writing, photography, videography, etc.).

The third blank answers the first of the main position questions, "What do you do?" This might include services such as websites, logos, book designs, poster designs, product designs, outdoor signage, product brochures, annual reports, or trade show graphics. (Resist the urge to use "branding" as your service since it's so vague and commonly used).

The fourth blank answers the second main positioning question, "Who do you do it for?" Pick only one industry. For example: independent healthcare providers, plastics manufacturers, renewable energy companies, elder care facilities, real estate agencies, local banks or credit unions, trade associations, beverage manufacturers, and so forth.

The fifth and final blank answers the third positioning question "How does it benefit them." This might be the hardest to answer. Since this is a made-up exercise you may not have actual experience in these practice areas, or in these industries. So for now just make stuff up—you're creative, use your imagination.

Next, take one of the three sample statements you came up with and try to create a list of five blog posts you might write that demonstrate a familiarity and insight into that area (a title and brief description is sufficient for each item). Feel free to make stuff up, so long as the content would clearly support the premises of the positioning statement. Here's an example.

_____[Grant Design]_____ is a ___print designer___ that produces ___collateral materials___, for companies in the ___wealth management___ industry, so that our clients gain ___prestige at every touch point___.

Here are some blog post ideas for such a design practice.

- Why wealthy clients respond to the feel of quality, handmade papers.
- How to make a strong impression using old printing techniques.
- Why the wealthy still love their business cards.
- Send high-end business card holders (filled with your cards) as client thank you gifts.
- How foil debossing creates the feel of luxury.
- The gift of bookplates conveys prestige.
- For wealthy clients, lead with print, and make the web all about convenience.
- Break the rectangle, die cutting connotes elegance.

I have no idea if any of those things are true. I simply imagined myself as someone who did print collateral for wealthy clients (or clients whose market is the wealthy) and made stuff up. If I were really focused on that area, I would easily be able to come up with many more ideas for content. You would never fake content, of course, but the point of this exercise is to show how a focused positioning makes idea development so much easier—and enables your content to bolster the claims of your positioning.

How Narrow Positioning Facilitates Prospecting

Not only does narrow positioning make content strategy easier, it also enables you to find prospects.

So let's assume you've chosen a narrow position, and you've updated your website to clearly communicate your new focus, and you've written a handful of blog posts that begin to express your professional insights about how your services benefit your clients. Now you need a tactical marketing plan to find and win new clients. The hardest part of implementing your plan is done: you've identified what you do, who you do it for, and why it benefits them. Now you simply have to start making contact with prospects. And for that you'll need a few basic tools.

In the old days, making contact with prospects was much harder than it is today. Resources for identifying prospects were mainly printed industry directories, and matches needed to be typed into databases, or spreadsheets, and contacting them involved regular old snail mail or cold calls. Today, with data sources like LinkedIn, Crunchbase, and numerous other industry-specific databases, finding prospects is the easy part.

Finding Prospects with LinkedIn

My suggestion for finding prospects is to start with LinkedIn. It is, by far, the most robust, complete, and well-known system, and its advanced search and filtering tools make it simple to identify people and companies at a granular level. You can search by industry, by role in organization, by geographic location, by company size, and other filters.

> *My suggestion for finding prospects is to start with LinkedIn.*

And now that you've identified your positioning statement, you should be able to search by industry, size, and role, and get a great list of prospects to begin reaching out to! In fact, let's take one of those sample positioning statements from our exercise and try to generate a list of prospects in LinkedIn. One way to know that your positioning statement is narrow enough is that it becomes very easy to make a list and find your market. If you're still having a hard time making a list, it's probably because your practice statement is still not narrow enough.

An Additional Benefit to Prospecting with LinkedIn

Another attractive feature of using LinkedIn for prospecting is the "someone's viewed your profile" report. Have you ever logged into LinkedIn and been notified that certain people have viewed your profile? Out of curiosity, don't you look at their profile in return? When you do this, they also get notified that you viewed their profile. You can take advantage of this subtle dynamic. While you are researching prospects you will trigger a number of return profile views. Your Linkedin profile therefore should be ready to take advantage of that. Make sure you link to your latest content, and express your positioning statement on your profile! Additionally, you might respond to their view by making a connection request or InMail them to see if there's anything you might be able to help them with. It's a bonus return on your marketing research efforts that's unique to LinkedIn's platform.

There are a couple of things to keep in mind when prospecting on LinkedIn. If you narrow down a list of potential prospects within your targeted industry and if your search results generated more than one thousand potential prospects, if you try to navigate to the end of such a list you'll find that you can't view profiles past the one thousandth. So when you are doing searches that you will ultimately want to add to your CRM, make sure that you use enough filters to keep any specific list under the one thousand profile viewing limit. Geography can usually be used as a segment to get any set of lists under that limit.

With LinkedIn, finding potential prospects is the easiest part of the process. But once you've identified a set of prospects that would be interested in your services, you need to start the more toilsome effort of adding them to your CRM and reaching out via email. And for that you'll need a couple more tools.

Tools of the Marketing Trade

Choosing a Customer Relationship Management system (CRM)

You're going to need to choose a CRM to maintain your growing list of potential prospects, organize them into segments, stages, and statuses, and keep track of the efforts you make in reaching out to them.

SalesForce is by far the most popular CRM on the market, and it is a robust platform. However, for the freelance artist or designer, SalesForce is probably overkill and overpriced. There are many others to choose from. I've used SalesForce, Insightly, BaseCRM, and Copper, but my go-to platform today is Hubspot CRM. Hubspot offers a wide range of inbound marketing tools and services, and while you may consider opting in for their whole suite, they also offer just their CRM solution for free—unlimited contacts, unlimited users, for an unlimited time. And comparing their CRM with the others I've paid for, it's just as good, if not better. One advantage Hubspot has (in addition to being free) is that almost every other marketing platform or online service you might use will likely have a native integration with Hubspot. And that makes integrating your website, email sending platform, and CRM so much easier.

One caveat to using Hubspot, while it's nice of them to offer it for free, they do this, of course, in the hopes that you will want to add some of the paid features to your account. Once you opt in for one or more of those features, your costs will be scaled based on the number of your contacts. And since a good prospecting database should aim to include at least three to five thousand contacts, those costs can start to add up.

Another thing to keep in mind when evaluating and implementing a CRM is that most CRMs are geared to sales automation. That's why the most popular CRM is called "Salesforce." And so some of the main features of a CRM will focus on sales pipelines and sales team interactions. CRMs have highly developed flows to track the stages of prospects from New, to Working, to Nurturing, to Closing, to Client. And likewise they track deals and opportunities through similar sales pipelines. For high volume sales teams these CRM functions are critical. But for the freelance creative, or even for the creative services firm, those features are not really needed, or at least minimally employed. So don't get too caught up in that aspect of evaluating CRMs, instead look at the ease of use, and ease of customization for managing your contacts and companies.

Choosing an Email Marketing Platform

Just like the CRM market, there are many email marketing platforms to consider. The most commonly used are Mailchimp and Constant Contact, again because they both offer a freemium model. Mailchimp has a native integration with Hubspot, so that's a plus. When evaluating other options, you should be aware of a couple of things. Most of the more advanced (and more expensive) platforms offer email automation. Platforms such as Activecampaign (which I use and recommend) and Infusionsoft allow you to trigger follow-up emails on a schedule, or based on the actions or inactions of a prospect. Used poorly, they are the bane of all who get spammed with "Just following up on the email I sent you last week" messages. But used intelligently, these platforms can be powerful. Honestly, for the creative freelancer doing basic outbound emails to get their content strategy rolling, a nonautomated platform like Mailchimp is going to be sufficient.

One other thing to keep in mind when you're evaluating email platforms, and other non-CRM marketing platforms—is that they all offer their own "CRM" capabilities. But in almost every case I've seen (and I've seen a lot of them!) the CRM aspect of these services do not compare with the capabilities of a true CRM that offers custom fields, strong faceted and filtered searches, custom column display and ordering, and so forth. So you'll probably need both a true CRM and an email platform and use native integrations to keep them in sync.

Designing Your Marketing Workflow

In order to build a marketing workflow, you'll want to identify a few steps and stages in reaching out to prospects. This would include having a basic email template ready. It should be short, to the point. Your "cold email" should not tout your abilities and talents, but how what you do benefits them—that third part of the positioning statement. It's also a good idea to provide them with a simple way to follow up and learn more. Obviously, going to your website is one action they might take, but it would be even better if you directed them to a particular blog post or

Keep your cold email short, simple, and to the point

project that would be most relevant to them. But keep your cold email short, simple, and to the point.

Sometimes a simple email is enough to draw a prospect to your website which can lead to inquiry or opportunity. But your marketing plan needs to take timing into consideration. Even if you hit your target, and identify a prospect that is well-suited—and they may even see the fit themselves, your timing may be off—their needs may not correspond with the timing of your outreach. So you should have a follow-up plan. Perhaps ask them to add their email to a newsletter list. Or at least tag them with a follow-up reminder in your CRM, so you can touch base a few months later to remind them of your services.

You'll be designing a set of stages of activity for yourself, and for how you contact and respond to your prospects. Don't get too locked in on this process. You're going to change and adjust it often as you learn what works and what does not. But whatever you set up to begin with, and however you adapt it, the key is to stick with it. Set some reasonable goals. Perhaps you commit to forty-five minutes per day, four days a week, with the goal of adding at least ten new prospects a day to your contact list. If you do that every week, you'll soon have hundreds of contacts to work with.

In the early days of your marketing you may need to commit more time to this activity. But as you make progress and build your reputation in your industry, eventually you'll find that your reputation precedes you and that prospects find you rather than you having to search for them.

On Networking

Most books on marketing include or even emphasize networking as a part of your marketing plan. I have a few reservations about this. And, as you might predict by now, it has to do with how positioning fits into networking efforts.

Generalist Networking: Proceed with Caution

You can learn a lot from other freelancers, especially as you're first getting started. They can offer you a glimpse of the practicalities of the road ahead—what it's like to work from home, how to write proposals and invoices, how to get health benefits. But unless they, too, have narrowed their own positioning, you might also hear about the challenges that you'd like to sidestep. So if you are at the beginning of your freelance career and you're trying to tap into your professional network, pay special attention to matters of business development and overall quality of work.

You might hear stories about months-long stretches without any work at all, pounding the pavement and knocking on doors until at last an opportunity presents itself. Think of how much energy must have been spent chasing the wrong leads, how much time and money was spent on coffees, and then ultimate disappointment of taking on work that doesn't satisfy your creative needs. What if, instead, these freelancers were spending their time building lists of qualified leads, filling their websites with focused content, and only taking coffees with prospects whose needs fit their services? They may have still gone months without working, particularly at the beginning, but once they landed that first gig doing what they set out to do in the first place, they would be firming up their positioning as an expert rather than a plug-and-play resource.

Networking vs. Industry Conferences and Speaking Engagements

It feels logical to do all of your networking locally, particularly if you've been in your area long enough to know a lot of people. But the point of narrow positioning is to focus on a vertical, not just a location. So how do you network with the right people in the right industry if they're spread out all over the country?

Chances are, the industry that you want to serve has national or regional conferences that you could attend. Most of these conferences have dedicated vendor halls where you can rent a table and try to attract new leads with flashy signage and bowls of candy. But this is not what I am suggesting you do.

When you attend an industry event, go as if you are an active participant of that industry. Because, if that's your positioning, that's what you are. Sit in on panels, meet people over coffee breaks, ask smart questions. The money you'll spend on going to a conference might be a little high, but if you consider the number of local coffees you'll be able to skip, it might very well be worth it.

Better yet, look for opportunities to speak at conferences in your chosen field. If you have an expertise that is needed in a particular industry, you might be able to propose a talk or form a panel that isn't just useful to the attendees, but bolsters your own reputation in the space.

So if you network, do it strategically.

Chapter 7: MARKETING
Summary and Assignments

1.   Where do you fall on the artist/artisan spectrum? Are you afraid to commit to focusing in just one area of creative services and in one main industry? What will it take to get you to be willing to do this?

2. What kinds of marketing efforts have you made in the past? Have any of them worked particularly well?

3. How would you describe the difference between "sales" and "marketing?"

4. Watch *Jiro Dreams of Sushi* and *Crafted* for inspiration in forming a narrow positioning.

5. Write your three sample positioning statements.

6. For each sample go to LinkedIn and see if you could easily search for prospects based on that focus.

7. For each sample try to come up with a half dozen or so possible blog post ideas that would demonstrate insights into that area of expertise.

8. Write a short email that might be used by a creative professional with a specialization from each of your samples to prospects in that industry.

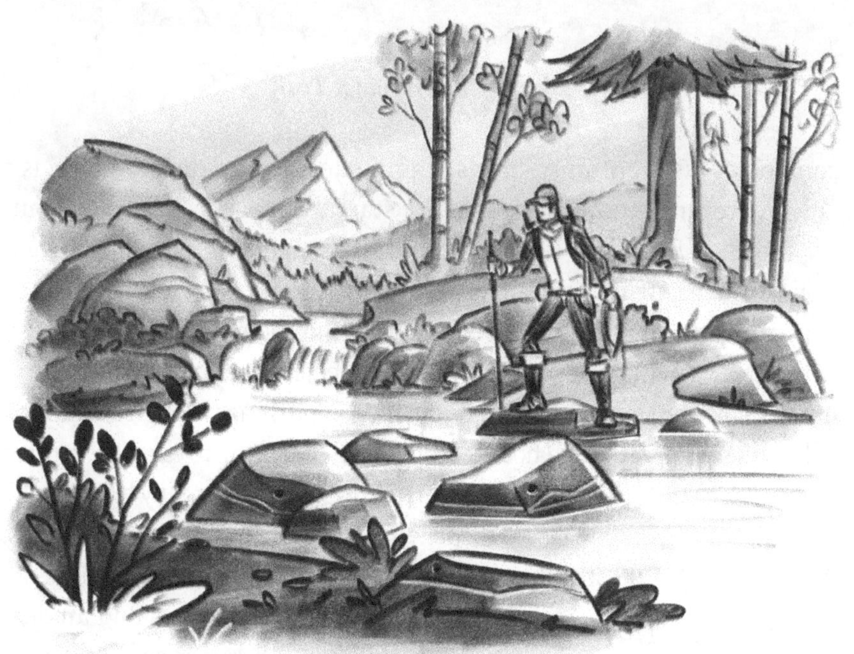

Chapter 8: MINUTES in Practice

As we've been blazing a new trail down the other side of the freelance mountain, we've laid out the particular challenges of managing all the various roles you have to fill as a solo creative entrepreneur. We've also pressed hard for that all-important commitment to narrow positioning. Once you get a handle on managing your practice well, you'll find that one of the rewards from that toil will be greater control over and freedom of your time. We'll get into the details of Money in the next chapter, but time and money are closely related and when you operate profitably you will not only have a growing bank account, but also more control over your time.

But here's the challenge: Until you get those things in order, you have to invest even more time implementing these practices until they start to bear fruit. Every entrepreneurial endeavor has overhead. That's why startup founders spend so many hours in their business in its early stages. And creative entrepreneurship is no different. But how you spend those hours and whether your efforts are driving toward stability and control, or just spinning wheels digging deeper and deeper holes, is a chief factor in whether your creative startup will succeed or burn out.

So as we move into evaluating how to manage your minutes, this tension between getting a grip on your time while having to spend even more of it on implementation, will be felt here too. But there is a special challenge in the area of managing your minutes. You see, it's one thing to work extra hard during the startup phases of a business—pushing through the burden of late nights and weekend hours—and it's another thing to carry the burden of knowing exactly how many hours you're spending as you are making these changes. Quantifying and evaluating your time can add an extra level of stress and anxiety to an already high-stress season. Often entrepreneurs write off the fact that they are spending an inordinate amount of time on their business in the hopes that success will bring change and relief. But without tracking, measuring, and analyzing their time, they can create distortions in some of their evaluations. If these distortions are not corrected, they can perpetuate unprofitability and instability. And so while it can be an added burden to an already time-intensive season of work, keeping and measuring your time is critical. This information will become the primary source of data you'll need in order to get your time back under control.

> *Evaluating your time can add an extra level of stress and anxiety to an already high-stress season.*

How Much Time Do You Really Have?

One of the biggest mistakes freelancers make in allocating their time is that they assume that most of the forty to fifty hours they work in an average week can be spent doing billable tasks. But in reality *you will not be able to maintain more than 60% of your available work hours* for billable project work. And if you don't plan on giving at least 40% of your time to maintaining your business, you will end up working many more hours than you ever planned. Worse, if you neglect the nonbillable aspects of your business, it may lead to the closing of your business all together.

To understand why you can only count on 60% of your time for billable project work, we need to see what takes up the other 40%. And keep in mind, the 60% includes all client communication, meetings, and planning—not just time sketching, designing, writing, and producing. If you do anything that you would not otherwise be doing, if you did not have that client, it needs to be recorded and captured under the 60% billable category. The nonbillable 40% does not include *client* administration and communication—that's always part of the 60%! Rather, the 40% is made up of tasks related to running and maintaining your creative practice itself: office administration, reviewing financial reports, evaluating time reports, professional development, and most importantly, implementing your marketing plan.

So let's break this time allotment down, and work through an exercise of blocking out a typical week. Here are our parameters. We're going to assume a 45-hour work week. So using our 60%/40% benchmark, that gives us 27 hours for billable client work, and 18 hours for all other tasks. Let's break these hours down into some hypothetical allocations. (These are not meant to be definitive standards or even guides—they just show all the kinds of things you'll need to do in a week, and how they might contribute to your overall time usage.)

Billable Project Time (60%):
    Project work—20 hours
    Project coordination—3 hours
    Client communications—4 hours

Overhead Time (40%):
    Financials—2 hours
    Time recording/review—2 hours
    Professional development—1.5 hours
    Office tasks (clean up, buying supplies, etc.)—0.5 hours

Email and administration—2.5 hours
Estimating new projects—1.5 hours
New business follow-up—4 hours
Marketing—4 hours

Now these will probably not be your actual allocations, and, of course, every week will shift time from one category to another. But remember, if you leave one of these tasks off, you're going to have to make it up the next week. Patterns of neglect in a particular business area will cause real and growing deficiencies in your practice. So if you can't get to your finances, or new business tasks, or marketing because of a pressing project—you'll need to give it back the next week. Otherwise, you will either neglect important aspects of running a profitable company, or you'll end up burning extra hours trying to catch up, which is unprofitable and unsustainable.

This rough allocation probably won't reflect your actual weekly breakdown. So let's do an exercise where you block out a typical week plugging these allocations into a weekly calendar. Sketch out a weekly planning grid similar to this Google Calendar example. Start penciling in how you might fit everything in the list of tasks noted previously into a hypothetical week.

	MON 1	TUE 2	WED 3	THU 4	FRI 5	SAT 6
9 AM	Client Emails, 9am	Office Tasks, 9am	Client Emails, 9am	Client Emails, 9am	Client Emails, 9am	Financials 9 – 11am
10 AM	Project 1: Client Call 9:30 – 10:30am	Client Emails, 9:30am	Marketing 9:30 – 10:30am	Project 2: Planning/Concepts 9:30am – 12:30pm	Estimating Projects 9:30 – 11am	
11 AM	Marketing 10:30am – 12pm	Marketing 10 – 11:30am	Project 2: Client Meeting 10:30am – 12pm		Project 2: Design 11am – 12:30pm	Time Review 11am – 12pm
12 PM		Project 1: Client Call 11:30am – 12:30pm				
1 PM	Project 1: Design 1 – 3:30pm	New Biz Call 1 – 2pm	New Biz Call 1 – 2pm	New Biz Call 1 – 2pm	New Biz Call 1 – 2pm	
2 PM		Project 1: Design 2 – 5pm	Project 1: Design 2 – 5pm	Project 2: Design 2 – 4:45pm	Project 2: Design 2 – 4pm	
3 PM	Professional Development 3:30 – 5pm					
4 PM					Projects: Status Review 4 – 5pm	
5 PM	Email/Admin, 5pm	Email/Admin, 5pm	Email/Admin, 5pm	Email/Admin, 5pm	Email/Admin, 5pm	
6 PM	Time Entry, 5:30pm	Time Entry, 5:30pm	Time Entry, 5:30pm	Time Entry, 5:30pm	Time Entry, 5:30pm	

Once you block out a week allocating time for each of the tasks and functions, maybe your model week might look something like our example calendar.

In practice, no actual week would ever work out like this. You might have just one new business meeting and, due to travel time, it might take up all four of your marketing hours. Or perhaps you take up almost the entire week focusing on completing a project. But when things like that happen, you'll need to allocate time in the following week to catch up on the marketing, new business, and financial tasks you skipped the week before. You can't put these things off forever without neglecting important aspects of your business!

Sketching out a theoretical work week will give you a sense of proportion for how each kind of task uses up your time. Of course, calendar sketches are just preliminary planning tools. But setting a baseline can help ensure that you're not neglecting important aspects of your business. Your model schedule will also provide some accountability. Think of this as a time-budget. Just like you have a financial budget and use it to evaluate your profit and loss statements, your model schedule will provide a standard for evaluating your actual time usage.

But it is only after you have collected sufficient data that you will be able to evaluate and adjust your time allocations more realistically.

How to Plan Your Week

A model schedule makes sure that you include adequate time for each important function of your business. In practice every week will be different. You might consider setting aside either the last or the first block in your weekly schedule to do a thirty minute review in order to plan out your time allocations for the coming week.

When planning an upcoming week, start with any items that are already fixed. For example, scheduled client meetings should already be in place. Then add in a few blocks for priority tasks that you know you need to give attention to and block them off your calendar so that you don't overlook that task or double-book the time. After working these items in, you'll start to see that some days are going to be more broken up than others. When you see that you have a day with three or four short meetings or administrative tasks, you might want to set aside that whole day for administrative matters. Spend some extra time clearing out your inbox, or assign some extra marketing in between the other items scheduled that day. Since few people are good at multitasking (and I'd argue that even those who think they are never do their best work under such conditions), never try to do deep work like writing or producing on these fractured administrative days.

Once you start to see the shape of your week, and you've added in the immovable items and any priority time allocations, start to look for days or half days that seem fairly clear, and set those times aside for creative productivity. And once you block those off, you should do your best to keep them clear, and even perhaps communicate via voice-mail message or email autoresponder that you will be unavailable during those times and will get back to clients soon after. That will help you keep those times focused and you won't need to worry that you are missing any important client communications.

Getting into healthy planning and scheduling rhythms brings regularity, stability, and control into the management of your practice. But to get proficient at planning, you need to get a realistic handle on how much time it takes to perform the various tasks involved in running your business, not to mention for budgeting and estimating project work. That's why it's important to evaluate how much time you spend on marketing, finances, and administration tasks—in addition to project time. That's why you need to commit to implementing and using a time-tracking system.

Tracking Every Minute

To evaluate your time usage you need accurate time records, so make a commitment to timesheets. Let's consider some basic principles for implementing an effective time-tracking system.

Completeness and Accuracy

First of all, you need to gather *all the time* you spend at work, every minute—not just the time you spend on billable projects. I can't emphasize this enough. Your timesheet data needs to do way more than tally up billable hours for invoicing. Time analysis is supposed to give you a complete picture of where *all your time* is going. And this is important because it's your nonbillable, internal, or client support time that puts the most downward pressure on your profitability. You need to see where all your time is going to recover areas where it is being wasted or uncompensated.

You need to gather all the time you spend at work, every minute.

Not recording all time in every category will corrupt this valuable resource of time data. Missing hours or days, or missing categories, will end up painting an incomplete picture. Another way of corrupting the data is by *discounting your time* when reporting it.

Underreporting your time on particular tasks will paint too rosy a picture. We're tempted to fudge and underreport our time when we think that we spent too long, or when we're going over our estimate and budget on a project. Doing this only perpetuates problems. We need to be sober-minded about our capabilities and how long it takes us to do things. We can't take ourselves "off the clock" just because a project is going over budget. It's better to see exactly where your time went off the rails, and learn from those experiences, than to write off that time. Unless all your time data is intact, your next project estimate may repeat the same deficiencies. So capture every hour spent. No "off the clock" subsidies allowed!

Completeness is important, but so is accuracy. In order to maintain accuracy, enter your time as close to the expenditure as possible. Minimally, you should enter your time at the end of each day. Ideally, you should be tracking as you go—or at least jotting down start and stop times throughout the day. If you neglect to fill in your timesheets at least daily, you'll find yourself fudging them at the end of the week. It's hard enough to accurately recall the details of a day's work at the end of one day, and even more so at the end of the week. Unless your time data is accurate, it will do you little good when it comes to analyzing and learning from this valuable resource.

Tracking time can be a pain. But it is not impossible. And while every minute does need to be accounted for, you do not necessarily have to measure by the minute. Rounding off your time into fifteen-minute intervals is sufficient. Between using fifteen-minute intervals and being diligent to record or enter your time daily, this task can become a simple rhythm to your work day. Another way to keep your time tracking as easy as possible is to maintain a clear and concise set of time categories.

Logical Timesheet Categories

Since you need to track and record every minute of your day, you'll want to make this effort as simple as possible. There are plenty of automated tools available out there, but the tools are only as good as your ability to use them. Making any system work requires carefully setting up your categories.

Every time system will include some obvious and basic data entry fields. These include date, client name, project ID, description, billable/nonbillable flag, and of course, the amount of time spent. But in order to use a time system efficiently and effectively you're going to need to give some careful thought to your timesheet *categories*. If you have too many categories and subcategories, or if you are inconsistent in their use, entering your time will be cumbersome. And more importantly, evaluating your time will be convoluted. You should be able to get by with no more than a dozen or so categories and subcategories.

The main fields in a timekeeping system (date, client, billable/nonbillable, time spent) are self-explanatory. But the work categories require more planning. Since you'll be using this data for evaluating project performance, as well as a resource for building more accurate quotes, these categories should be primarily meaningful *for those purposes.*

It's worth investing sufficient time thinking about your workflow and your *project phases* in order to formulate your categories properly from the start. You don't want to have to change these categories very often. Whenever you do, it will become difficult to connect old time data with new categories. And not to beat a dead horse, but when it comes to establishing and maintaining a useful set of categories, having fewer areas of service, and repeating the same kinds of work, which come from narrow positioning, will not only make establishing these categories easier but also using and analyzing them.

Here are some suggestions to get you started. They may not match your process, but they should serve as a model for how to think about your categories.

The Importance of Project Phases

One of the limitations I've found in many time-tracking systems is the lack of support for project phases. Breaking your process down into phases is helpful for planning, budgeting, and scheduling, but it's also helpful for efficient and insightful time evaluation. Since some systems don't support project phases, you may need to create multiple projects related to each other using a careful naming scheme.

Here is an example of how a design project might break down into phases (with discrete tasks within each phase).

Discovery Phase:

- Planning
- Research
- Strategy
- Procurement (lining up needed resources, [i.e., photography, art, technical partners])

- *Discovery Phase Communication and Administration*

Creation Phase:

- Concepts
- Design/Draw/Shoot
- *Creation Phase Communication and Administration*

Production Phase:

- Art/File/Photo Preparation
- Packaging and Delivery
- *Production Phase Communication and Administration*

Follow-Up Phase:

- Changes, Adjustments
- *Follow-up Communication and Administration*

Note that in my examples each phase has a distinct subcategory for *Communication and Administration*. This is a better approach than having one overall category for communication. That's because, once you start tracking time, you may be surprised at how much is used in communication and administration! Finding ways to be efficient in communication is one of the aspects you'll want to work on to improve your business. Isolating where communications tend to escalate will be helpful information. You may also want to note, in your description field, the kind of communication involved (phone call, email, meeting, etc.).

If your time system does not support breaking projects into phases (and most don't), you'll have to create unique projects or tasks for each phase using a common job number as a key linking them together into one overall project. For example, if you were doing a brochure for a client named Progress Scholastic you might give that project a code like PS001. You would then create the following projects (based on the suggested project phases above): PS001:Discovery, PS001:Creation, PS001:Design, PS001:FollowUp. You would then create categories matching the various tasks within each phase.

It's a good idea to have at least one category called "Other" so that you can record unusual tasks that don't fit into one of the established categories. But when you use an "Other" category, try to make sure you give those entries more robust descriptions so that you can evaluate them later.

By setting up a clear set of project phases, and categories that define the main tasks involved in each phase, you will make entering your time much easier.

Nonproject Phases

Since it's critical to record all your time spent on the business, not just project billing, and since you will spend 40% or more of your time on nonclient work, you should track and evaluate administrative time as well. Setting up helpful categories, that will shed meaningful light on your time usage without being too complicated, is critical in this case too. Here are a few suggested categories with explanations that you might want to consider for tracking your nonclient time.

General Administration: A category for basic daily things like cleaning up, office management, and the random, distracting YouTube video can be a helpful catch all, but should be kept to a minimum—remember you're your own boss and you're always watching.

Communications: Remember, each project phase has its own project-related communications category. Project communications is always a billable category and has to be tracked to the project. But sometimes you'll have communications relating to running the company itself, and this would be a place to track that time.

Marketing: This is a key category to plan for and use well. Once you have a narrow position you'll need to bolster and demonstrate it. That will involve writing and creating content, planning marketing campaigns, and constantly evaluating and sharpening these efforts.

Business Development: When your marketing pays off and you have a lead, you'll need to spend time communicating with them and writing some form of proposal or statement of work. This time should be kept separate from general communication and marketing. Marketing leads to sales, and the efforts involved are distinct.

Finances: We'll discuss the details of managing your money and your cash flow in the next chapter, but you need to set aside at least a couple hours every week to manage your finances. Any less frequently and the chore will become so oppressive that you may avoid it all together. And if you do keep it up once per week, it will be efficient, and any transactional anomalies will be easy to clear up since there is only one week's worth of recent transactions to review. One other reason it's important to track the time you spend on finances is that it is one of the first roles a freelancer might seek to outsource to a bookkeeper. But you may find that it only takes you an hour or so each week. And the value of listening frequently to what your money is saying can provide valuable signals for your decision making. Outsourcing might not save much time or money, and you'll lose the insight you gain by simply keeping up with your accounts.

Professional Development: If you go to professional development seminars or conferences, or spend time learning new skills, this is the place to record that time.

Planning: Sometimes you need to set aside time to think about the big picture, to consider the overall state of your business and where you want to take it. Setting aside time for this and tracking it will give you data to see whether or not you're giving adequate attention to the big picture.

Time Off: Completeness of your data is critical. However many hours you plan to work in a week, all of them need to be fully reported. The easiest way to confirm that you've done this is to scan back in time and make sure that each week's hours are fully recorded. If you don't record time off, that missing time will leave holes in your data. Those gaps will make it harder to recognize if you failed to record time. Entering time off, so that every week has forty or more hours recorded, can help ensure that you are collecting comprehensive time data.

Project Coordination

Accurate time data will help you estimate future projects, and establish realistic project schedules. But even the most accurate schedules with perfect time allocations for every task will fail if you don't proactively coordinate your projects, particularly when client input, review, or feedback are involved.

There are many project management and task management systems available (Basecamp, Jira, Monday, Teamwork, Wrike, Mavenlink, and so many others). They are all helpful, almost essential. But regardless of which system you use, the responsibility to proactively plan and communicate project meetings, milestones, dependencies, reviews, and feedback deadlines with your clients rests with you. If you don't take this important role by the horns, you can count on delayed projects, client reschedulings, and late feedback that derail projects, create bottlenecks, and stack up deadlines.

While it doesn't take a lot of time to send email reminders about upcoming meetings, it does take advance planning and proactivity. After every meeting you should follow up with suggested times for the next planned meeting and get it on the calendar. You should send out reminders a week ahead of a scheduled meeting and again a day or two before.

Careful project coordination will not eliminate every delay, but it will minimize them. And when you show careful and deliberate effort to respect the time of others, your clients will learn to respect your time as well. If you don't, then you can count on your clients to be loose with your time, and not respect your deadlines. (Though they will most certainly hold you to theirs!)

Your clients will learn to respect your time.

One way to start off a new client relationship well, particularly with getting them to respect your time, is to ask them for any blackout dates for their team when they know in advance that certain days or times will not work for responding to a project plan and schedule. If they have planned vacations or major company events that will make them unavailable, get them into your overall project schedule from the start. Not only will this make your schedule more realistic, it also establishes an expectation that your time matters and that the schedule is important.

Project Status and Completion Evaluations

Using past data for quotes and schedules is important. But having complete, accurate, and up-to-date time information will also help you manage your current projects more effectively. You should know how your projects are proceeding as you work through them. You need to know when you are going over budget, and when you are on track (or even better, to know when you're coming in under budget thus improving your profit margin!). This means that you not only have to keep your time system up to date, *you also have to look at your performance regularly.* I would recommend setting aside about an hour per week to view reports for all your ongoing projects and track time spent against the remaining project's budget. A good time system will include basic reporting features which should make this analysis easy.

When you review your projects and discover a problem (like approaching the end of the budgeted phase when there is still a lot more work to do!), you'll need to investigate. Is that overage an anomaly? Is it related to client changes? Or were you not on your game that week? Do you need to make some adjustments to your process? Perhaps you need to budget more for that phase when quoting future projects. These kinds of observations are where you learn so much about your workflow and process. Without tracking and evaluation, you might never learn these things and, therefore, never improve. This is another reason for weekly evaluation. It's so much easier to recall where things went wrong over the past week than months later when your recollections are fuzzy.

One last thing to review each week is your ratio of billable to non-billable time (looking for something close to that 60%/40% split). If you're regularly less than 60%, then you are going to have profitability problems. If over 60%, you're probably neglecting important business management tasks, and that might lead to strong billings in the short run, but they come at the expense of your long-term health.

Weekly evaluation gets you the most gain. But also don't neglect long-range planning. Set aside extra time, perhaps quarterly and annually, to do deeper evaluations—looking at longer periods of time. Some trends may only reveal themselves when stepping back and considering impacts over months and years.

Which Budget to Measure Against?

Your weekly evaluations compare your time spent on a project, or project phase, with its budgeted amount. But keep in mind, there is a big difference between how you represent a project budget in a proposal to a client and how you actually work. So you are going to need to translate every client's proposal budget into an internal budget that reflects your project phases and actual workflow. The bottom lines of these versions need to match, but how you present your budget allocations to a client, and how you measure them doesn't have to be the same (so long as you come in on budget).

Your internal budget will be more detailed and accurate in ways a client might not be able to understand. For example, your communication and administrative time allocations for a project may use upward of 25%

of an entire budget. Not many clients would sign off on a proposal that included a 25% administrative fee. Yet, in reality, it takes a lot of communication to deliver good work. So while in your proposals you might distribute that time into other phases, your internal project schedule will properly reflect the real world allocations to the communication and administration tasks in each phase.

Choosing a Timekeeping System

Back in the day, gathering and reporting time data was a ton of work. Paper timesheets had to be manually entered into Excel files or a Filemaker database, and custom reports produced. But with all the web-based applications available today, this is so much easier! I'm a big fan of Harvest (getharvest.com). It's relatively inexpensive at about twelve dollars per month for a solo user account. They also have an optional, integrated project planning system called Forecast. Forecast is to time data what your cash flow projections are to your money. I have not seen anything quite like it, and in my opinion it is a killer feature over the other options.

Toggl.com is also a popular system, probably in part due to their free, single-user option. Most project management systems offer built in time tracking capabilities. Using those features has the benefit of linking your time to your project schedules. Unfortunately, those options generally have a poor user interface and may lack a mobile option. Since commitment to timekeeping already faces so many barriers, I'd go with the system that is easiest to use, and not let poor access or poor interfaces present yet one more barrier to consistent use.

There are many other timekeeping tools available. You'll want to find one that allows for both browser and mobile access—so you can easily log time on the go. But make sure that whichever system you choose that it provides good reporting capabilities. These reports are the whole point of tracking your time in the first place!

Chapter 8: MINUTES
Summary and Assignments

1. Consider all the main project and business tasks that go into your typical work week. Identify which ones are client related (billable tasks) and which ones are overhead. Calculate how many hours will pertain to each group using the 60%/40% benchmark standard against the total number of hours you intend to work each week. Then assign a benchmark number for each kind of task. Use a blank weekly calendar to sketch out a sample week that provides proper allocation for every task.

2. If you are not currently using a time-tracking system, pick a product and begin to use it. Getharvest and Toggl are two safe choices. At the end of each day, make sure a full day's time is always accounted for. And at the end of each week, make sure that the whole week's time has been entered.

3. Evaluate your project processes and try to break them into a few discrete phases. Then think through all the tasks associated with each phase. Try to keep the total number of categories around a dozen or so.

Too many and you'll make time entry too complicated. Too few and you won't be able to do meaningful analysis.

4. Pick a time each week when you will ensure all your time is accounted for, check to see where you performed relative to the 60%/40% utilization benchmark, and evaluate where current projects stand relative to their budgets.

5. Plan and schedule a day for sometime after you've collected at least six months of data for doing deeper analysis of your overall project patterns.

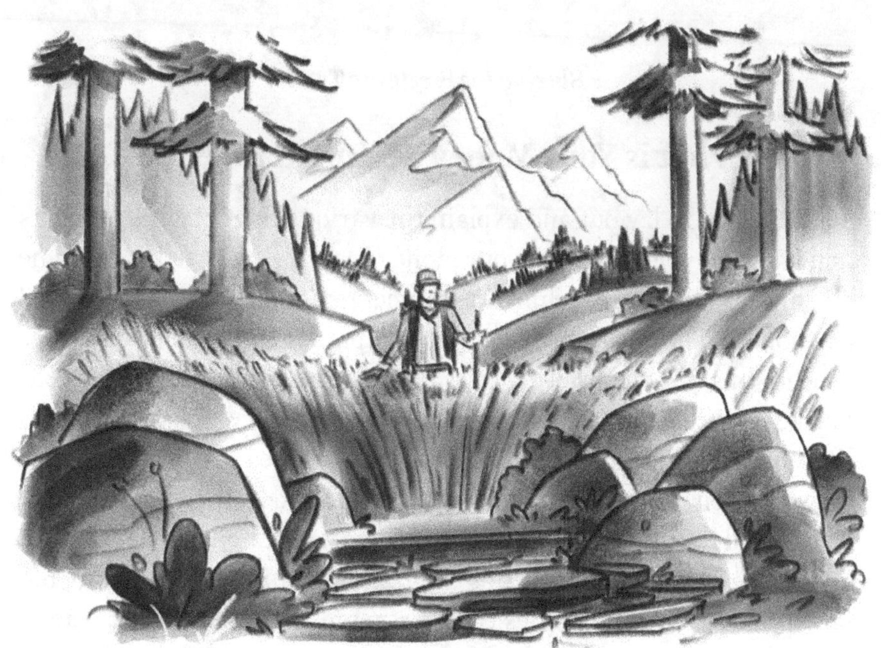

Chapter 9: MONEY in Practice

In the first chapter on Money, as we just began our trek, I discussed the uneasy relationship that creatives have with the financial aspects of running their practices. It's so important that this aversion be overcome, because when it comes to the nuts and bolts of running your practice, your money is going to be your most honest and dependable voice, not to mention that it really is the lifeblood of your business. If you run out, your business is dead.

But it should not be merely the fear of going out of business that motivates you to become adept at listening to your money. The rhythm of your financial transactions is like a heartbeat. It is the easiest, most accessible measure for your overall business health. If you gain the skills needed to manage your money, you will be well positioned for success.

But there may be one more reason that you fail to listen carefully to what your money is reporting to you, and that is, it may not have good things to say. Nobody likes to receive criticism, but if we do hear it and heed it, it can lead to needed and productive change.

What is Your Money Saying Right Now?

So as I begin to lay out and explain the various financial instruments that will help you hear what your money is saying, we need to set some baseline levels, some benchmarks for what represents a healthy financial position. And fair warning, when you compare your numbers with these benchmarks, you very well may discover that you're *operating unprofitably.* I make this prediction based on my knowledge that few creative practices are profitable. For most artists and designers, there is a considerable gap between their true value and what gets confirmed by their bottom lines. So we need to run some numbers to see if my educated guess is correct, and figure out if you're operating unprofitably. This may be painful, but facing your financial realities is the first step in solving the problems.

What Should Your Financial Targets Be?

Let's start with the biggest targets and the overarching goals that you should be aiming for. Then we'll take a closer look at some other more tactical targets like your hourly rate. The most important benchmark for the long-term sustainable health of your practice, as I've mentioned, is your *utilization* percentage.

The most important benchmark for the long-term sustainable health of your practice is your utilization.

Utilization. After you consider all the nonbillable business administration activity you will need to engage in, what's left are the hours you can utilize for billable project work. For the creative services profession, the typical upward bound for utilization, as pointed out earlier, is around 60%. There are many tasks you will need to spend time on besides your productive billable time. If you try to squeeze more billable time out of your week, unrealistically overestimating your capacity, you'll soon find yourself working nights and weekends to make up these necessary time commitments. Overworking is one way you might compensate for a lack of profitability. And if you don't fix that, your business will not be sustainable. You have to realize that running a business involves a lot of overhead. If you don't want to be limited to 60% utilization, you might want to reconsider your path and look for a full-time position—staff designers can hit upward of 80–90% utilization, spending most of their time doing design work as employees, rather than the lower 60% capacity of a freelancer.

As a consequence of the 60% utilization barrier, you'll need to set your hourly rate high enough to meet all your budget requirements within that 60% benchmark. We'll review how to establish an appropriate rate below.

Profit Margin: The next financial benchmark you should aim for is your overall profit margin. You should minimally aim for at least 15%. This should be built into every estimate or project quote. But remember, this is a minimum. You should work to increase your profit margin over time. Self-employed individuals need a large cushion of savings in case of a slowdown in new business, the loss of a large client, extended illness or injury, or the inevitable reduction of efficiency if you ever hire new employees. Profits can be set aside to cover these inevitable dips in productivity. Three to six months of operating capital is a safe foundation for a healthy business.

Compensation: If you're going to do the hard work of running a freelance practice, you should assume that there is a higher reward for your greater risk and effort. If you could make more money working for someone else, you probably ought to do that. Your compensation is the most determinative factor in setting your hourly rate. Again, I would urge you not to set your hourly rate based on your minimum sustainable income level. Too many expectations get established with clients based on your rates and quotes. If you build a client base off of a low rate because you can afford it right now, it will be difficult to get those clients to pay substantially more later when you need a higher salary. So set your compensation where you would like it to be, and establish your rates on that number, and build your client base on that. Don't burden yourself with lots of low-paying clients—and a reputation as the cheap option in your marketplace. Whereas the average range of staff designer salaries is between $30,000 and $60,000 per year, as someone running their own business, your minimum salary should be between $60,000–$90,000 per year.

Profitability Calculator

On my mentorship website, I've provided a Design Firm Health Calculator (ericholter.com/design-firm-health-calculator). This calculator is built for a small firm to measure their overall health; but by changing the number of employees to "1" it will work just as well to take your freelance practice's financial temperature. If you do not yet have an accounting system that can generate basic financial reports, you may have to do some digging to determine the exact values for the calculator.

By the way, many freelancers opt for simple and limited financial systems like FreshBooks, Wave, or Kashoo. These are great for general invoicing, but they are not fully featured accounting systems—they lack robust financial reporting features that genuine accounting systems like QuickBooks offer. My recommendation is to bite the bullet and invest in QuickBooks. It will require a learning curve, but in the long run, you'll have financial skills that will allow your business to grow and scale. Also, your accountant will thank you.

For now, if you're not sure, just guess at the values. But to get an accurate picture of your practice you'll need to figure out the real values from your financial records. Now, if you're just starting out in your practice, and you don't have real historical values to plug in, try out a few different scenarios, playing around with the inputs to see where things end up. This can help you to establish more realistic expectations and goals for your future efforts.

Let's review the fields in the calculator, what they mean and how they reflect your financial health.

Total Annual Revenue: This is your gross earned revenue for the past year, the whole nut, everything you earned.

Cost of Goods Sold: If you are a web designer, you might not have any cost of goods sold because pixels are free. But if you are a print designer, and you front the money for printing costs and get reimbursed by your client, these hard costs need to be deducted from the **Total Annual Revenue** amount. So put the total amount of pass-through revenue in here.

Earned Revenue: This field is the automatic calculation of your **Total Annual Revenue** less your **Cost of Goods.**

No. of Employees: As a freelancer, this value should be "1." However, if you ever bring in contract help, then estimate how much their contribution would amount to in terms of another full-time employee. Adding a fraction of an employee is fine, so if you use about twenty hours per month of contract help that would be about .125 employees. Or, it may be easier to find out how much of your **Total Annual Revenue** you spent on contractors, and add that amount to your **Cost of Goods Sold.**

Weeks Worked Per Year: Everyone takes time off. Deduct your days off per year (including holidays). If you're not sure, take a guess.

Average Hours Per Week: Don't fudge! If you don't have actual timesheet data fix that, but for now enter in your best guess of the average hours you spend at work each week. But make sure you account for everything you do for work—not just the time you spend working on projects! If you spend time on any task that you would not be doing if you were not running your practice—that counts as hours worked in a week.

Target Hourly Rate: This is the rate you bill out or that you use when estimating projects.

Utilization Percentage: This is that important number. As stated it should be around 60%—the percentage of hours that can be captured against paid projects, in contrast to the time you spend on the business itself.

With these basic inputs, we can start to get a read on your financial health. The calculator will evaluate your inputs and provide the following results.

Your Effective Rate Should Be: This result calculates the rate you entered, times the total hours available for work in a year, and adjusts it by utilization. This number shows the potential amount of money, per hour, you could be generating for every hour you are "at work." It's lower than the full rate you charge because it takes into account the reality that you can't capture every hour, that there will be administrative overhead. But if you hit your targets, this value shows you the real amount of money your business generates hourly. The simplest way to use this number is to compare it with what you might be able to earn working for someone else (who would pay you for all your time spent at the office regardless of whether or not all your work was "billable").

Your Effective Rate Actually Is: This may be a painful number to look at. The first value, **Your Effective Hourly Rate Should Be,** is hypothetical and doesn't measure it against your actual financial performance. But based on your **Total Income** minus **Cost of Goods Sold,** and taking the other inputs into account, this is what you are netting out per hour working for yourself. If this rate is not substantially higher than what you could earn working for someone else, you have a real problem.

Your Actual Utilization Is: As indicated above, a healthy practice should aim for 60% utilization. Your **Actual Utilization** is the number of hours you capture for productive billing. If it's lower than 60% closing this gap becomes one of your financial performance goals.

Rate Differential: This is the difference between your actual and effective rates. This is how much more you can be earning, per hour, if you close your utilization gap. This may be a painful gap, but keep in mind that if we fix this, you will be making that much more money per hour without working any additional hours overall. But it is also the money you are losing each hour that you continue to work under unprofitable circumstances.

Potential Increase In Revenue: This is the hopeful number. It represents what you could be earning without working any more hours than you already are. You will have to work differently, and close the gaps in your utilization. But as you move in that direction this is money you can gain—without hiring, and without working more hours.

So, what did the calculator say? Do you have some room to improve? I thought so. The two main ways to improve your current profitability are to increase your rate and close the gap in utilization. That's a simple prescription, but getting there may take a lot of work.

What Should Your Target Rate Be?

Closing the utilization gap is one critical way to improve profitability. Raising your rates is the other. But what should that rate be? Another calculator available on ericholter.com is the The Freelance Rate Calculator (ericholter.com/freelance-hourly-rate-calculator/). This tool takes all the relevant factors into consideration in order to provide *a minimum rate* you should be charging. Additionally, this calculator compares what you should be charging with your actual effective rate based on some of the same inputs from the previous calculator. That rate is likely going to be lower than the rate you should be operating under. But exactly how much lower is the rate you capture compared to the rate you bill out? Are you ready to find out? Let's go to the Freelance Rate Calculator. This might sting a bit.

> **Desired Salary:** This number is entirely up to you. If you're just starting out, it might be lower than you'd want it to be in the coming years. However, I want to encourage you to aim high here. As a business owner and not an employee, you are taking risks. The higher the risk you take, the greater the reward ought to be. Also, even though you might be content with a fairly low salary today, keep in mind that raising your rate later after your clients have become accustomed to your lower rates can be difficult. So it's better to start with a long-term sustainable rate from the get-go.
>
> **Weeks You Work Each Year (47 typical):** As in the previous calculator you need to account for your time off, vacation, holidays, and sick time.
>
> **Average Hours You Work Per Week:** Also, like the previous calculator, you need to establish your preferences for the number of hours you plan to work each week. Be conservative

here. The fewer hours you input the higher your rate will need to be. You can always choose to work more hours and make more money in a particular week, but you don't want to lock yourself into having to work lots of hours just to make ends meet.

Uncompensated Hours Per Week: This input is similar to the utilization percentage in the last calculator. Again, it ought to reflect the 60% utilization benchmark (although this field is asking for the uncompensated hours rather than the utilized hours). So if you are going to work a typical 40-hour week, and your target reflects the 60%–40% split, you would put 16 unpaid hours into this field.

Desired Profit Margin: You have to plan your profit into your rate. Fifteen percent ought to be a minimum margin. But again, I'd encourage you to aim high.

Business Expenses: Every business has fixed costs, overhead, consumables, and professional expenses to cover, things like software and computer equipment upgrades, online fees (LinkedIn, QuickBooks, etc.), marketing expenses, travel expenses, professional services, professional development, and office expenses. This is a rough breakdown of what some of these items may consist of for the average artist or designer. They don't cover everything, and so if you have additional expenses, add them into the "other business expenses" field.

The calculator totals up your desired salary, adds in your expenses, includes the desired profit and then displays the total income you would need to meet all those goals. Based on those numbers, and the amount of time you indicated that you would ideally like to spend in the business, the calculator gives you a minimum hourly rate. Now if you're brave you can compare your desired outcomes with your actual performance. Enter your actual current revenue, your actual weeks worked per year, and the actual number of hours you work in a week. This will generate the actual comparable hourly rate you're earning. What's the bad news? Could you earn more than this comparable hourly rate by working for another firm? Like it or not, this is what you're earning. Let's hope it's at least higher than the minimum wage!

Getting to Know Your Financial Instruments

It's time to get down to some financial basics. You're running a business, you need to understand your basic financial reports. We're going to look at five, three of which you will need to look at regularly. But in order to even begin using these instruments, you're going to need to start using full-featured bookkeeping software. As mentioned earlier, lightweight invoicing systems like Freshbooks and Wave don't provide the kinds of financial reports you're going to need. I recommend Intuit's QuickBooks online. It's by far the most popular, and you will be able to easily run your reports. You'll probably need training and some support and there are many QuickBooks training options, including support from Intuit, courses on LinkedIn Learning, and many YouTube videos. My website, ericholter.com, also offers subscription-based training videos including detailed walk-throughs for setting up and using QuickBooks (among other training videos). While QuickBooks is designed to do more than the average freelancer needs, and thus may seem a bit overwhelming at first, once you get familiar with its basic functions, it's not difficult to keep up with. And once you do, you will be able to easily run important financial reports—reports that are unavailable on those more limited invoicing systems.

You're running a business, you need to understand your basic financial reports.

Once you have all your accounts in QuickBooks, there are only three or four parts of your accounting system that you need to be familiar with.

1. Chart of Accounts: Your chart of accounts includes all your financial vendors (bank accounts, credit card accounts), your asset and liability accounts, as well as the various income and expense categories you use. When you start using accounting software, there will be a list of typical income and expense accounts already set up for you. You can always customize this list, add and remove items, or rename categories, but I would suggest doing this sparingly. The more your account categories match the standards, the easier it will be to work with financial advisers, accountants, and bookkeepers.

You will need to have a firm grasp of what each of the categories in your chart of accounts is used for—so that you can easily and consistently assign your revenue and expenses to the correct categories.

2. Budget: You should establish an annual budget for each income and expense category you use. NOTE: Unfortunately, in QuickBooks, the budget feature is only available in the most expensive version which, at the time of this writing, is about $40 per month (the starter plan is closer to $20 per month). Putting your budget into QuickBooks allows you to easily evaluate how each of your expense and revenue categories is performing against your planned budget.

When you are first setting up your budget, unless you have historical data to inform this process, don't worry too much about getting each line item perfectly accurate. Make your best guess. Your actuals, over time, will help you set better, more realistic budgets. Start with your best guess and work from there.

3. Profit and Loss: Your P&L, sometimes called an income statement, is one of the most basic financial instruments you will use. It simply lists what you have earned and spent in each of the categories listed in your chart of accounts. You can pull reports that show your income and expenses month-by-month, quarterly, or annually. The nice part of having the budget feature enabled in QuickBooks is that you can include it as an additional column in a P&L report to see which categories are over or under budget. Another reason you want to be familiar with your chart of accounts is so that you can readily understand your P&L reports. If you find any significant variances from budget, you can click on the category and review all the transactions to see why you are going over budget.

Once you are using an accounting system, running and evaluating these reports is quick and easy. Within a minute you can pull a report, scan the latest results, making sure everything is in bounds, and then get back to work. Without an accounting system, it could take hours to process bank statements, categorize, and generate reports—which means you'll never do it. And, therefore, you'll be making business decisions in the dark.

4. Balance Sheet: The balance sheet is another basic financial instrument, but this one gives you a different perspective on your finances, and it is more confusing to non-accountants. But it's your balance sheet that is going to give you the "bottom line" about your financial health (though formally this bottom line is the second to the bottom line of the report—go figure). The P&L report shows the accumulated income and expenses broken down over time. Your balance sheet is more like a snapshot of your overall performance as of the date of the report. Your balance sheet tells you the theoretical cash value of your company as of the date on the report. If you were to cease operations at that moment, this report tells you what your company would be worth. The line of the balance sheet that gives you this number is called "Total Equity." It is the second to last line in the report. If all your accounts are up to date, the total equity is what your company would be left with, if you were to close up shop that day, sell your assets, and pay your remaining bills and debts. Hopefully, this is a positive number. And if you are profitable, *it will be a growing number.*

Because a balance sheet is a snapshot in time, you need to be careful about how you use them. Your total equity line can jump up or decline significantly from one day to the next. For example, if you run your report on Tuesday, but then on Wednesday you receive a payment (if you run it in cash mode), your equity will go up. Or if you pay a large bill on Wednesday (and you hadn't entered it into the system) it will go down.

So there are a couple of rules of thumb when evaluating your total equity. First, try to run these reports around the same time of the month—ideally after you've made all deposits and paid all your monthly bills. Secondly, balance sheets are most useful when you compare the total equity trends month-by-month. If your company is profitable, this number should trend upward (even though you may have an occasional down month). If this number stays flat, or trends downward, you are simply not profitable. You may need to evaluate further why you are not building your equity (value) into the company—but these numbers don't lie. If your total equity does not grow, you have profitability problems.

The structure and format of a balance sheet can be confusing. It's grounded in the basic accounting dictum that assets always equal liabilities plus owner's equity. Its historical purpose was to ensure that no mistakes or oversights existed in the books. If all accounts were in balance, then the accounts were sound. But if the total of assets were not in balance with liabilities and owner's equity they knew there was a problem somewhere. But you can ignore all that. For your purposes, what matters most is simply evaluating your *total equity* month-by-month, making sure that you run the reports under as similar monthly circumstances as possible.

5. Cash Flow: Of all of your financial instruments, your cash flow is the most important and most difficult to maintain. Therefore, we'll spend more time and go into more detail on managing a cash flow spreadsheet next. And just to avoid a potential confusion, QuickBooks has its own report called "Statement of Cash Flows," but that is not at all the same as what we will be reviewing here.

Managing Your Cash Flow

Managing your cash flow is more complicated than reviewing a P&L or a Balance Sheet because *predicting* cash flow is a somewhat subjective process. You can send out an invoice with a due date assigned, but how often do clients pay according to your terms? Also, when you start a new project you will get a partial deposit, which will infuse cash into your business—but you then have a lot of work to do to earn that money. On the other hand, when you've completed the work, you may have to wait some time before you receive that final payment. Sometimes projects are broken up into several progress invoices connected to key project deliverables. Reaching those key project markers is sometimes dependent on client feedback and approvals. And if your client falls off the face of the Earth, failing to provide timely approvals, your project will stall. (Isn't it annoying how clients can be so fastidious in holding you accountable to all your project due dates, but so much more for-giving and flexible when it comes to their scheduled input?) If you've been at this a while, you know that the only predictable thing about project schedules is that they are unpredictable. And so when your invoices are tied to progress deliverables, your cash flow will likewise suffer some unpredictability.

Because of these realities, a useful cash flow management system is going to have to be *flexible*. And accounting software is anything but flexible. Therefore I recommend using flexible spreadsheets to effectively forecast your short-term receivables. I've developed a sample spreadsheet for this purpose that you can use and modify to fit your needs. Go to ericholter.com/cash-flow-template and you will be prompted to create a copy of the spreadsheet in your Google account.

What Are Cash Flow Problems, Really?

Before we dive into the details of this cash flow spreadsheet, we need to acknowledge a plain truth about cash flow. *Cash flow problems are the result of profitability problems.* Profitable firms rarely experience cash flow shortfalls. If you experience regular cash flow struggles, that's one more confirmation that you're not yet profitable. And so this spreadsheet is a tool to help navigate the cash pressures that small design practices deal with as they process monthly payments against anticipated project revenue. It will allow you to predict and adjust for the cash flow pressures you'll face as you slowly grow from a position of unprofitability to solid profitability.

Cash flow problems are the result of profitability problems.

Not only does this cash flow spreadsheet track invoiced receivables, it also aligns them to your monthly expenses. And this is critical, because cash flow measures the dynamics between your receivables and your payables over time. You have to align both to get an accurate read.

While there are plenty of resources for getting basic bookkeeping training, tracking your cash flow is more difficult, especially since design projects are usually invoiced in parts according to project timelines. You'll need to get a handle on your invoicing and predict the timing of your receivables and try to balance them with other expenses as they come due.

While the main goal of managing cash flow is to simply make sure you never run out of funds to cover your expenses, as you'll see, in managing your cash flow, you'll gain other important insights into your financial performance.

With cash flow, timing is everything. A late payment on a large project can seriously impair your cash flow. When you map out your expenses and expected receivables, over time, in your cash flow spreadsheet, you will be able to see at a glance how far out your revenue will cover your expenses. If you have a positive forecast for two or three months, you're doing quite well. If your projection shows a negative for the current month (and those following), you're not in good shape, and you're probably stressed out!

The Cash Flow Spreadsheet

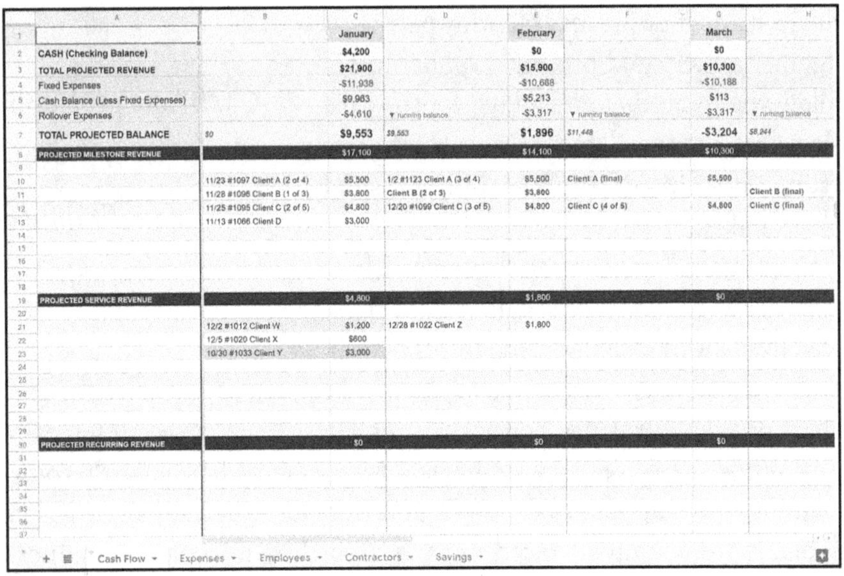

	A	B	C	D	E	F	G	H
			January		February		March	
2	CASH (Checking Balance)		$4,200		$0		$0	
3	TOTAL PROJECTED REVENUE		$21,900		$15,900		$10,300	
4	Fixed Expenses		-$11,938		-$10,688		-$10,188	
5	Cash Balance (Less Fixed Expenses)		$9,963		$5,213		$113	
6	Rollover Expenses		-$4,610	▼ running balance	-$3,317	▼ running balance	-$3,317	▼ running balance
7	TOTAL PROJECTED BALANCE	$0	$9,553	$9,553	$1,896	$11,448	-$3,204	$8,244
8	PROJECTED MILESTONE REVENUE		$17,100		$14,100		$10,300	
9								
10		11/23 #1097 Client A (2 of 4)	$5,500	1/2 #1123 Client A (3 of 4)	$5,500	Client A (final)	$5,500	
11		11/28 #1096 Client B (1 of 3)	$3,800	Client B (2 of 3)	$3,800			Client B (final)
12		11/25 #1095 Client C (2 of 5)	$4,800	12/20 #1099 Client C (3 of 5)	$4,800	Client C (4 of 5)	$4,800	Client C (final)
13		11/13 #1066 Client D	$3,000					
14								
15								
16								
17								
18								
19	PROJECTED SERVICE REVENUE		$4,800		$1,800		$0	
20								
21		12/2 #1012 Client W	$1,200	12/28 #1022 Client Z	$1,800			
22		12/5 #1020 Client X	$600					
23		10/30 #1033 Client Y	$3,000					
24								
25								
26								
27								
28								
29								
30	PROJECTED RECURRING REVENUE		$0		$0		$0	
31								
32								
33								
34								
35								
36								
37								

+   Cash Flow ▾   Expenses ▾   Employees ▾   Contractors ▾   Savings ▾

The sample spreadsheet includes five tabs. The first is the main Cash Flow tab, the second is for Expenses followed by Employees, Contractors, and Savings.

The main Cash Flow tab is broken into pairs of columns for each month (each month has one column for invoice descriptions and one for the amount of the invoice). The Total Projected Revenue calculates the total revenue expected from the various invoices listed in each month, less the expenses expected over that same period of time which tells you how much cash you will have at the end of the month, assuming that you receive all the invoices anticipated and pay out the expenses allocated for that month. Hopefully, you have a positive number for the current month, and if your company is profitable, you should expect to see a positive number for a few months out. Well run practices might see a positive cash flow projection for as many as four or five months.

There are a couple of other structures built into this cash flow spreadsheet. The invoice sections are divided into Projected Milestone Revenue, Projected Service Revenue, and Projected Recurring Revenue invoices. You may or may not want to maintain those distinct categories. The basic concept is to use the Projected Milestone Revenue section for larger projects (those that will be broken into two or more progress payments). Smaller, quick turnaround projects (ones that would be billed all at once) are placed in the Projected Service Revenue rows, and any recurring revenue, perhaps retainers or maintenance contracts, would be listed in the Projected Recurring Revenue rows.

Modeling Receivables in the Cash Flow Spreadsheet

The art of managing your cash flow is in being able to predict when you will actually receive the payments from the invoices you list in this spreadsheet. It's one thing to send an invoice "due upon receipt," or "net 30." It's altogether another thing to get those checks in within that time frame! Some payments are easier to predict than others. You might realistically expect to receive an initial deposit for a new project in a timely manner. But that final project payment may be a long time coming. Also, you will get to know which of your clients process payments regularly and which ones require reminding (a task no one likes to do!). Getting good at maintaining an accurate cash flow document requires experience, and knowledge about each client's payment patterns, as well as continuing your efforts to communicate your payment policies.

It is extremely important to maintain *consistent* and *conservative* habits in forecasting your expenses and receivables in this document! Be warned, the pressure and stress that comes from a lack of profitability, and its result, negative cash flow, will incline you to get overly optimistic about receivables, pulling them forward into the current month to cover current expenses—or push off expenses that are not absolutely due right away. This tendency is the result of denial that you are suffering from a serious lack of profitability, and if you don't correct it, and stay realistic and consistent in mapping your receivables, you'll end up deluding yourself into thinking that your cash flow is better than it is. So if you send an invoice with net 30 terms, place it into your cash flow as if it were net 60. Always assume the payments will come a little later than you expect, rather than sooner. If they do come sooner, great! But don't create stress for yourself by overly optimistic projections.

Planning Receipt of Milestone Invoices

In the cash flow spreadsheet sample, notice that some entries are bolded. Those bolded items represent progress payments that have not yet been invoiced (thus they do not carry an invoice number like the others). But since you plan on making progress on the project, such that you can expect that payment within the month you're projecting, you'll want to represent that in your spreadsheet. This is one way a spreadsheet is better than your accounting system for cash flow prediction. Your accounting system can only report on invoices that have already been created. Unless you create partial project invoices in advance, these payments would not be reflected in an accounting system. Keeping your cash flow spreadsheet up to date will also serve to remind you to send invoices as you approach milestones for each project.

Of course your invoice assignments in the cash flow document are just projections. As you know, if a project gets delayed by a client, those payments may need to get pushed off into later months. When that happens you copy and paste or drag and drop the invoice into the next month. You may also notice that some sample invoices are in red—those represent final payments. They are distinguished from the rest because of all your progress payments, final payments are the hardest to predict. Clients hold off on paying those last payments until they are entirely satisfied that all the work they wanted out of you has been delivered.

All these invoices are tallied and totaled in the top rows, and the expenses subtracted for the balance. But for this to be an accurate representation of your cash flow, your expenses also need to be kept up to date.

Earned vs. Unearned Revenue

An important dynamic, with respect to modeling your receivables, is the distinction between *earned* and *unearned* revenue. When you receive your first payment for a new project and deposit it in the bank, those funds have not yet been earned. You still have a lot of work to do before you reach a new project milestone and send your next invoice. Depending on your invoicing and payment practices, when you get that next payment, it, too, may be unearned. In contrast, when you send a final invoice at the completion of a project, that revenue is fully earned.

One common mistake that distorts cash flow projections, is confusing earned versus unearned payments. When you deposit a check from a client, your cash balance in your checking account goes up. But does that mean you're now more profitable by that increase in your balance? Not at all. The cash is an asset, but you have to offset your assets with your liabilities before you can know your bottom line. (This is essentially what a balance statement shows you.) But whereas a balance statement will adjust your checking balance by adding back in any liabilities such as credit card balances or other debts, a balance sheet can't tell the difference between a deposit that has been fully earned versus one that has not been earned.

There is a real hard dollar cost to your time. And that cost is a liability that needs to be set alongside any unearned payments you may receive before you can know what, if any, profit there may be in that cash. The labor needed to

There is a real hard dollar cost to your time.

earn the revenue you've already received is a corresponding liability that neither your balance sheet, nor your cash flow will reveal.

Confusing earned versus unearned revenue is a key mistake designers make when evaluating their profitability. It's why they sometimes can't understand why, if they are working so hard, they are having cash flow problems. It's because they already got paid, perhaps long ago, for the work that they are doing today. They're still in the process of earning the revenue they've already received and spent. Depending on your billing practices, particularly if you bill half up front and half on completion, these distortions can be considerable. And unfortunately, these pressures cause a freelancer to chase after more new business in order to meet current cash needs—to get a new deposit on a new project to cover costs. But, of course, that deposit will also be unearned and will need to be earned with future labor. Thus designers kick the "profitability can" down the road. Sadly, if this problem persists, the mounting need for more labor to earn the revenue they've already received might suggest that they need to hire help. But if their increased workload is not an indication that they are successful, but rather the effect of unprofitability manifesting itself as an unearned revenue problem, hiring can be a catastrophically bad decision.

One way to avoid this problem is to try to keep your receivables as close to the time when you've earned the revenue as possible. This can be accomplished by breaking your projects up into more frequent milestones. Fifty-fifty billing creates the maximum earned versus unearned revenue distortion. Billing in thirds, fourths, or even greater fractions will help to reduce these distortions.

Modeling Expenses in the Cash Flow Spreadsheet

Just as unearned revenue is a liability that needs to offset any payments you may receive, there are other liabilities that need to be tracked alongside your receivables. Therefore you'll find an "Expenses" tab in the cash flow that looks like a basic budget. In fact the default values should reflect your budget (which you might have in QuickBooks as well). However, the expense tab is also broken up into specific months so that you can align the timing of receivables with your monthly costs.

You may need to change the particular rows to represent your actual budget and expenses. But you'll notice that the expenses are broken up into a few categories. These categories are not grouped by type of expense, like most budget worksheets. Rather they fall into two main groups: "Fixed Expenses" and "Rollover Expenses," and both are broken down even further.

The "Fixed Expenses" section is divided up between "Credit Card Expenses," "Monthly," and "Compensation." Credit card expenses and monthly items are distinguished from each other since credit card expenses have to be paid all at once, whereas you might have more flexibility on the payment schedule for all your other monthly expenses. The "Compensation" section pulls in values form the "Employees" and "Contractors" tabs.

The "Rollover Expenses" section includes two sub-categories, each of which include expenses that do not occur monthly, but that will come due at some point during the year; your accountant's bill, for example. But these are broken down monthly because you need to be factoring in these costs over the year so that you do not get surprised by spikes in expenses when they arrive. The first sub-group is "Rollover Retained" for expenses that you will roll the accumulating amounts over into each month, until the amount comes due. The second group "Rollover Transferred" lists typically larger annual expenses that you will transfer into savings each month. (You can use the "Savings" tab to keep track of these transfers.)

These "Rollover" expenses are separated from the fixed monthly expenses because while you should plan for them, if you have a shortfall, they could be postponed, or possibly, if they are optional they can be eliminated. Professional development expenses, computer upgrades, and such should be included in your budget, but if you have a shortfall, you can simply decide not to save for those areas in a particular month.

Getting back to our main "Cash Flow" tab, notice that the top lines show your cash flow balance before and after counting your "Rollover Expenses." That's so that you can evaluate your cash flow keeping that softer category for flexible expenses in view.

Lastly, notice the "running balance" fields in the column next to each monthly total. This adds the previous month's balance to the running month's since the balance for the current month will rollover into cash as each month ends. This running total helps you see the overall impact of your revenue and expenses over time. (Note: When you close out a month and delete the expired month's column, you will need to manually set the value of what will become cell B7 to zero. That's because the running balance cells need to reference a value there in their running calculations. So when you first delete a past month, the running balance totals will temporarily show a #VALUE! error. Change B7 to zero and the running balances will be restored.)

A cash flow spreadsheet is the best dashboard you have for real-time tracking of your performance.

Without a doubt, maintaining your cash flow spreadsheet requires more work than running a P&L or a balance sheet. But it also gives you the most comprehensive view of your short-term financial situation. Getting familiar with these categories, and getting used to keeping it up-to-date may take some time. But once you get it down, a cash flow spreadsheet is the best dashboard you have for real-time tracking of your performance.

Keeping the Cash Flow Spreadsheet Up-To-Date

Now that you're familiar with all of the elements of the cash flow spreadsheet, let me walk you through the process of keeping it up to date. Before you update cash flow you might want to do your basic, weekly QuickBooks updates first—downloading all your bank and credit card transactions, categorizing each item, and reconciling each account. By the way, you should never mix your personal financial accounts with your business accounts. Take the time to set up a business checking and savings account and business credit card.

After updating your accounts, open up your cash flow document. The first thing you'll want to do is update the "Cash (Checking Balance)" cell with the current updated balance. Important tip: before making any updates to cash flow, jot down your cash flow spreadsheet's *current balance* for a few of the upcoming months. After updating deposits, removing the corresponding invoices, and deleting paid expenses, that balance should be close to what it was when you started (unless you've added in new invoices or new expenses). If there are any big discrepancies, you may want to take a closer look. There's nothing worse than increasing your cash balance and forgetting to remove an invoice that has already been deposited. Such errors can cause serious distortions to your cash flow. Fortunately, Google Sheets has a robust version history feature for not only the whole sheet, but for individual cells as well. So if you get really confused you can always start over, or look back for where an error may have occurred.

Next, update the various invoice entries. Have you received and deposited any payments this week? Delete those from the document—the value of those is now reflected in your updated bank balance. Additionally, whatever expenses cleared this week should be deleted from the Expenses tab. By the way, keeping your Expenses tab updated also serves as a reminder to pay all your bills every month. If you delete each amount as you pay them, then even if you misplaced a physical bill, the fact that the expense is still listed will serve as a reminder that you still need to pay that bill.

Now you want to add new entries. If you have new bills that you have not paid, you should update any placeholder amount in the Expenses tab with the actual amount of the bill. Likewise, if you have cut any new invoices, they need to be added to the list. As you review the list, you may notice that it's time to send out invoices for those bolded place holders. If so, cut the necessary invoices, add the invoice number to the entry, and unbold the item. It's also a good idea to add the date that you sent the invoice so that you can see at a glance those invoices that are overdue. Place that item in the month you realistically expect to receive it (remembering the doubling rule—if your terms are "net 30," put it out sixty days). This will create the most up-to-date view of your cash flow status.

Weekly Updating

It will take some doing to get trained and acclimated to an accounting system like QuickBooks. But once you are, you need to make a *firm commitment* to keep up with your books. My advice is to commit to spending at least an hour *every week* to update your accounts, reconcile your statements, and do your invoicing. You should update your cash flow even more frequently, every time you receive a payment or pay a bill at least. In my experience, if you do not commit to doing this *at least weekly* you will end up not doing it at all. And if you try to catch up every couple months, it will be such an arduous task that you will not want to do it again for a very long time.

Maintaining your finances weekly may take about an hour or so. But if you do it less frequently, it won't add time incrementally to the process; *it will multiply the time.* That hour of financial updating may expand to three hours if you wait two weeks. That's because each transaction you enter needs to be assigned to its proper category. If you update weekly, then every transaction will still be fresh in your mind. But the longer you wait, the fainter your memory of each transaction, requiring more time to track them down.

So pick a time each week, maybe a Saturday morning, or a weekday evening, after the phone has stopped ringing, when you can take an hour and get all your accounts and transactions up-to-date.

The discipline of regular bookkeeping not only keeps your information accurate and up-to-date, the more you stay on top of your financials, the more clearly they will be speaking to you. And whether they tell you good or bad news, those conversations will help you make better decisions as you navigate your business.

Maintaining the Cash Flow Spreadsheet Year over Year

The sample spreadsheet I've provided has one year of receivables and expenses modeled in it. But you'll need to extend the columns as the year progresses. I suggest that at the end of every quarter you add the next quarter to the end of the document. These new columns need to be added to both the cash flow tab, the expenses tab, and the contractors tab if you use that.

Should You Just Hire a Bookkeeper?

You need to get your finances in order, and ideally into a full-featured accounting system. But this is one of those tasks that can be outsourced. You can hire a bookkeeper to do this. And that might be the best choice, particularly if you need to switch over from another system. Bookkeeping services are not terribly expensive. Hour for hour, you can earn more focusing on your creative work than on balancing the books and reconciling your accounts. And if you feel like you don't have the mind for this kind of detail, maybe that would be for the best.

However, even if you hire a bookkeeper, you still need to have them run monthly P&Ls and balance sheets for you—and you need to look at them and understand them! Additionally, since your bookkeeper will not be able to maintain your nonstandard cash flow spreadsheet, you'll need to at least manage that key document yourself.

But before you punt, and look for a bookkeeper, I want to encourage you to consider making the effort to master this stuff. If you plan on sustaining your practice for the long-term, and if you think you might even want to grow into a small firm someday, then you should own the fact that you need to get your head around these standard financial skills and reports. You need to gain a basic competence running and maintaining your finances. The financial structure of most freelance creative practices is not very complicated. There's no inventory, rarely are sales taxes involved, no employees, and no payroll issues. And so while getting your head around QuickBooks will take some effort, it is doable. And once you get over the learning curve, maintaining your books really doesn't take long. By keeping up with your financials, you'll gain

By keeping up with your financials, you'll gain deeper insights into your business

deeper insights into your business—and that knowledge is well worth the effort.

So if you decide to dive in, you're going to need more training. For basic QuickBooks training, I'd suggest taking a weekend course, or an online training course from LinkedIn Learning. You might also want to consider becoming a subscriber to my training videos at ericholter.com. I cover QuickBooks, cash flow, CRM systems, email systems, and more—all specifically focused on deploying these systems for the creative entrepreneur. Another way to get acclimated to QuickBooks is by jumping in and kicking the tires with a sample company. QuickBooks maintains a sandbox demo account that lets you click around and make changes to a fictional company, so that you can get your bearings with their system (qbo.intuit.com/redir/testdrive).

Invoicing: Putting Weight on the Trust Bridge

As already mentioned, it's a healthy practice to break up your projects into as many milestone invoices as possible. This keeps your earned to unearned ratios close to reality. It also makes collecting on invoices easier. Clients are more willing to pay smaller, more frequent progress invoices than they are to making large bulk payments when work has not been demonstrated.

In every client relationship, there is an exchange of trust that takes place across the duration of a project. At the start, the client is making a big deposit in the trust account. They hired you, and are hoping you'll come through. They also cut a check to cover the deposit and first stages of work. You've done nothing tangible to prove or validate that trust. As you begin to deliver, assuming that the client likes your work, you will begin to earn that trust and relieve any anxiety they may have felt at first. But every time you send an invoice, you put new pressure on that trust bridge. So again, the more incremental those are, the less weight you put on the bridge, and the more trust grows naturally as the project moves forward.

By the end of a project, the trust account switches sides. That final invoice gets sent (or at least paid) sometime after you've done all your work—and now you are hoping that they pay up.

The worst thing you can do in establishing the trust bridge is to send an invoice too soon, or at a moment when the client's stress level may be high. Poorly timed invoices have often been the flashpoints that turn delicate projects into complete disasters.

One practice I've used is to tell my clients at the proposal stage that we send out our invoices thirty days (or whatever their payment terms are) *ahead* of planned milestone dates. This enables us to capture revenue close to the times when we've earned that revenue, which minimizes the earned/unearned distortions. But is also makes invoicing predictable for clients. And if there's one thing clients love, aside from successful projects, it's clarity and predictability in matters of money and invoicing.

Increasing Your Rates

One of the goals of narrow positioning is to find clients who will pay higher rates and fees because of your expertise. Establishing a narrow position does not mean that you jettison all your existing clients. But it does mean that if your old clients are going to stick with you (the ones you want to keep anyway), they'll need to adapt to higher rates and fees. There are some practical ways you can address the issues surrounding increases to your rates. And you should think about how you'll handle rate increases because if you wait until it's absolutely necessary to change your rates, you will no longer have the luxury of time—and changing your rates suddenly can create serious stress.

In order for your creative practice to grow, you need to maintain a healthy profit margin. And for freelancers this margin will come largely, if not entirely, from your hourly rate. Growing your practice will always involve additional costs and increased overhead. And so your rates will have to go up. But increasing your rates will upset the pricing precedents you've established with your existing clients and with your referral network. Significant changes to your rate may trigger existing clients to start looking elsewhere and prospects to be surprised by your fees.

Nevertheless, increasing your rates is a necessary part of growing a professional creative practice. And part of this progression will always include the acquisition of new (hopefully better) clients, and moving on from the old.

The Paralyzing Fear of Disappointing Clients

Transitioning clients to higher rates is hard for creative startups. Freelancers build close relationships with their clients. In fact, many freelancers make this a selling point: direct communication, personal attention, no middle-man. These are touted as advantages in hiring them as a freelancer. But eventually your costs will go up, and rates will have to increase, and clients will transition.

At a personal level, this is hard for a creative, because it's not just business. It's not just about necessary rate increases. It's knowing that your client Jane, with the twins, trying to run her gift shop, or Joe, the semiretired granddad, managing a nonprofit—that they will be negatively affected by your increase. And those are the hardest transitions. But, of course, you also probably have clients who can afford higher rates, but knowing a bargain when they see it, they keep you busy with lots of work—so long as they keep benefiting from your low rate. I hate to put it this way, but these kinds of barriers to building a creative practice come from the reality that most freelancers are just too nice.

The solution, of course, is not to be mean, or hard-nosed, but to simply become more professional. Professionals can be personable and nice. And if you can become more professional (which requires being profitable), then you can continue to help the entrepreneurial mom or the altruistic granddad. If you are genuinely profitable, then you can afford to willingly cut your profit margin for clients like these. But you need to be profitable first in order to have the time and money to give away (or discount). You can't keep giving away what you don't have, and working at unprofitable rates will eventually catch up with you. When it does, these clients will be equally disappointed—when you go out of business. If you're going to remain in business, you'll need to increase your rates.

And you need to do this proactively, intentionally, and in a planned way.

If you're going to remain in business, you'll need to increase your rates.

Timing is Everything

So if you wait to raise your rates until the moment you really need that extra profit margin (from having hired an employee, or adding overhead, or experiencing increases in your personal expenses), you will be way behind the inevitable transition curve that this change will require.

The fear of losing clients when you raise your rates might cause you to hesitate even longer to raise them. This will put you even further behind the curve. This is a downward spiral that has lead to the closing of many creative startups. You need to get out ahead of this curve, especially if expansion is in your future—either personally (mouths to feed) or professionally (adding employees). You can't wait until you must raise your rates to raise them. It can take a year or more to adjust your clients to new pricing structures. Some clients will adapt, some will leave, and some will be added, but not overnight.

Planning ahead is absolutely key for growing your practice. And planning for the jump from freelance to firm is one of the biggest changes to anticipate. Freelance rates tend to get pegged well under the one hundred dollars per hour mark. A design firm, on the other hand, should be charging one hundred dollars per hour at the bare minimum.

So if you are freelancing and considering hiring help, you should raise your rates to at least one hundred dollars per hour, well before you bring on your first employee. If you wait until after you hire you'll be at least a year behind the transition curve—and that will be a very stressful year. Rather, increase ahead of time and use the added profit from that increase to build a cash cushion that can be helpful in making the transition from freelance to firm.

How to Bring Your Clients Along

Some of your clients genuinely will not be able to pay higher fees. You may be able to keep a few of these, but you must count this cost and deem them worthy of your altruism. By keeping them, you will quite literally be subsidizing their work from your profit margins. If your client is a dear friend, or a cause you want to support, and you can afford to provide that time or money, then you may want to keep that client. But do not think of them as doing you a favor—helping to pay the bills or keeping the lights on. They are draining your profits, not providing a foundation.

By all means, be generous and give to them, if you have it to give, and want to do so—but do not consider them as a base or a building block.

Some of your other clients are bargain hunters and will not pay your higher rates or fees. When you raise them, they'll start looking for someone cheaper. Don't feel bad for that client. Part of their cost in hiring the lowest bidder means that they have to live with a lot of change. Freelancers regularly move on to full-time employment, or start firms that charge more. In the early stages they work cheaply, but the client who won't grow with them simply has to get used to continually finding new creative resources. These are clients you don't want.

On the other hand, you may also have clients that do want a stable relationship with you—a relationship they can count on. They value you as a partner that knows them well and they know this kind of quality partnership comes with a higher price tag—and good clients are willing to pay it. These will see your growth as valuable to them, and they will happily pay more knowing that you will be around to help them for years to come.

Some of your clients will be in the middle—not real happy about higher fees—perhaps not recognizing the value behind those fees—but willing to stick with you and pay the higher rates. In each of these cases you can make your rate transition smoother by planning ahead and communicating your goals proactively. Here are a couple of tactical ideas for moving in this direction:

1. State Your Goals at the Outset. When you bring on a new client, let them know that you intend to grow and build your professional practice into a strong firm. Tell them your general expectation on time frame. And tell them that you intend to raise your rates or fees along the way as necessary. Be frank. Let them know that you don't expect every client to transition with you, but that you will provide plenty of advance notice of changes in order to make them as smooth as possible. As a gauge, you might want to say something like, "I intend to raise my rates about $5–$10 per hour for every employee I bring on," or "You can expect a 5–10% increase in my rates annually."

2. Explain the Benefits to Clients. If you have not raised your rates in a planned and incremental way, and now find yourself facing your need to make a significant jump (say more than twenty-five dollars per hour from your existing rate) you may want to send your clients a letter explaining your business decision and underscore the value they will receive from the ongoing stability of your practice. Here's a sample letter you might use:

Dear Client,

We have been working together for several years. Thank you for your business! It is clients like you that have made our growth possible and enjoyable. As I have evaluated the profitability of my practice, I have come to recognize that our continued growth requires an increase in revenue across our entire client base. Growing from my freelance practice into a small firm has introduced roles, functions, and overhead that simply require greater margins to sustain us. As a fellow business owner, I'm sure you can relate. We hope that all our clients will see the value of maintaining a strong design partnership with us and see our growth and strength as a company as a long-term benefit to your brand.

Starting on January 1st we will be increasing our rate from $100 per hour to $120 per hour. We understand that some of our clients may need more time to reallocate their marketing budgets to cover our higher fees. Since you are a valued client to us, if you need time to adjust your budgets, please contact me and we'll see how we can make temporary accommodations for you.

We realize that not every client will be able to afford our new rates. We hope you are not among that number, but if you end up deciding to make a change, please know that we will cooperate with you in order to make the transition as smooth as possible.

Building a growing, professional creative practice will require increasing your rates. It is far better to plan for this, build it into your client development process, and lead your clients along, than to wait until lack of profitability requires unplanned and significant jumps. Don't be afraid of this natural progression. By being upfront and proactive with your clients in this regard, you will not only make the transition easier, but it also will position you in their mind as an even more competent professional.

Messages from Your Money

Money talks. Your finances have things to tell you. And while friends may sometimes flatter you, your money always tells it like it is. You may not like what it has to say, but if you listen, you'll start making much better decisions going forward.

Chapter 9: MONEY
Summary and Assignments

1.   Jot down your results from the two calculators. Use these as benchmarks for evaluating your progress as you close the utilization gap and establish rates (or quotes) that allow for a healthy profit margin.

2.   Lock in your new hourly rate, as optimally determined by the Freelance Rate Calculator. Commit to pricing that enables you to capture this minimum rate on all billable work.

3.   Sign up for QuickBooks Online or purchase the desktop version. If you haven't used QuickBooks before, sign up for an introductory class, take a LinkedIn Learning Course, or consider becoming a subscriber to my training videos at ericholter.com.

4. If you've been using QuickBooks or another full-featured accounting system, run a balance sheet and circle or highlight the Total Equity
line. File that report away so that you can use it to compare with next
month's report. Repeat monthly.

5. If you've been using QuickBooks or another full-featured accounting system, run a Profit and Loss statement for the past twelve months.
Format it so that it displays columns for each month. If you have the
budget feature available, include the budget for comparison. Evaluate
any accounts or budget line items that seem to be well outside normal. Is
that because of any miscategorizations? Or, are your income or expenses
not falling within planned ranges?

6. Download a copy of the Cash Flow Google Spreadsheet and customize
it for your use. Go to ericholter.com/cash-flow-template and you will be
prompted to create a copy of the spreadsheet to your Google account.

7. Establish a consistent time during each week that is least likely to
be interrupted for sixty to ninety minutes of financial updating. Do it.

Conclusion

So how are you feeling? A bit overwhelmed would be normal. But I also hope you're feeling hopeful and inspired to make some changes that will improve your practice. You will need to be patient with yourself. Implementing all of the processes, systems, and plans will take time. With diligence you should probably expect that it will take eighteen to twenty-four months to begin to see consistent fruit from your efforts.

It would be ideal if I were able to walk you through all this personally. There is no substitute for personal interaction, being able to ask questions, and getting a customized evaluation for where your energies should be focused. But since freelance practices rarely have the resources to engage personal mentoring, the principles in this book can help you to start moving in the right direction. You might also want to check out my subscription-based video training resources at ericholter.com. They go into even more detail than I can provide in print. They include step by step walk-throughs for setting up and using many of the systems referred to in this book.

But as you begin to set some priorities, let me share with you some of the things that you will probably need to put at the top of your list.

1. First, start tracking time. It's the easiest thing to do, it does not take a lot of time to set up, but the data you will begin to collect is a necessary resource for so many of your future changes, decisions, and adjustments.

2. Work on your positioning statement. This essential, yet difficult focus will become the foundation upon which you will control your marketing, improve your client base, and become profitable. If you are fearful, or hesitant, you might want to start with a "soft launch" of a new positioning. Use the three questions from the Marketing section, and establish an initial positioning statement. And simply start by committing to write one or two focused and meaningful blog posts about how your experience can help solve problems unique to your clients. Eventually you will want your entire website to boldly and clearly declare this positioning. But a set of consistent and focused blog posts and portfolio examples can be a good place to start.

3. Make sure your hourly rate is not undermining your efforts. Figure out what that rate needs to be, and start establishing your quotes and fees accordingly. If this key number is far off, you will continue to chase your tail, being distracted by putting out fire after fire that result from continuing to do essentially unprofitable work.

Your to-do list will be much longer than this. And your priorities may be different than these common starting points, but you need to start somewhere and begin to work diligently toward change, as you establish a foundation from which you can *Blaze Your Freelance Trail!*

Afterword

I wrote the initial manuscript for *Blazing the Freelance Trail* in the summer of 2016. In the fall of that year I changed directions from consulting to a full-time position as CEO and part-owner of Cuberis, a local web design shop that was one of my early Rewarding Toil clients. The owner had relocated to San Diego and needed someone to run and manage the firm. Based on my original consulting work with them they had chosen to focus on museums (and they already had a focus in website development). I got a chance to repeat my experience from Newfangled, my original company, and apply all these principles for Cuberis. That process is now well underway, but I'm freshly reminded how hard it really is, what an uphill climb it can be, to change and improve a creative practice in all five areas of Money, Minutes, Marketing, Management, and Motivation.

But I'm also freshly reminded that these principles work. If you listen to what your Money is saying, and give attention to how you spend your Minutes, if you commit to a bold narrow positioning, if you manage your efforts caring for each role, and if you can maintain your motivation in the face of many challenges, then a creative services practice can be highly rewarding.

About the Author

Eric Holter began blazing his creative trail while still in high school back in 1986. He ditched his grocery store job and hung out a shingle as an artist for hire. Then, a few years later, after graduating from Rhode Island School of Design in 1991, he began his professional career as a freelance illustrator. Soon after, he had an opportunity to acquire a letter-press shop, and so he added fine printing to his resume.

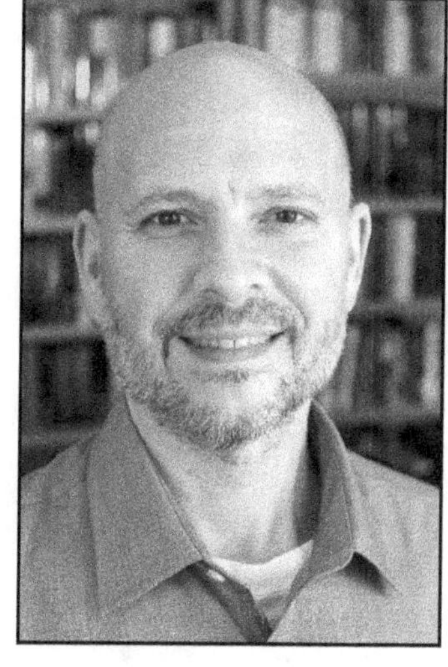

Shockingly, fine-press printing was not lucrative enough to support a family, and so he got a job in the city doing print production work at a local advertising agency from 1993–1996. In that short period, he experienced the radical transition from old-fashioned print production methods (stats, rubylith, photo type, paste-up mechanicals) to digital pre-press production. By the end of that brief era, his creative path diverged to follow after the newfangled world wide web trail and he started his first firm, Newfangled Graphics.

Newfangled is one of the few original web design firms that has survived both the dot-com bubble burst in 2000 and after 9-11, and is still in business today. Eric sold Newfangled to one of his employees and began consulting other similar firms in the business side of creative entrepreneurship. In 2016, the principal of one of his local consulting clients moved to the West Coast and needed a CEO to run his Durham, NC based web design firm, Cuberis.

Today Eric continues to oversee Cuberis, while mentoring other creative entrepreneurs, especially those just starting out down the trail, or beginning the ascent to hiring their first few employees.

You can find other articles by Eric Holter, as well as his podcast *5 Minutes on Creative Entrepreneurship*, and his subscription-based training materials at ericholter.com.